The Golf Swing

The Golf Swing

DAVID LEADBETTER

— with John Huggan —

FOREWORD BY
NICK FALDO

CollinsWillow
An Imprint of HarperCollins*Publishers*

To Kelly and Andy

First published in 1990 by
Collins Willow
an imprint of HarperCollins Publishers
London
Reprinted 1990 (twice), 1991

All illustrations in the book are
by Dave F. Smith

A CIP catalogue record for this book is available
from the British Library

ISBN 0 00 218350 1

Set in Janson by Ace Filmsetting Ltd, Frome, Somerset
Printed and bound in the United States of America
by Arcata Graphics, Kingsport, Tennessee

Contents

The author would like to thank
David Frost for his valuable help in
the preparation of the illustrations.

Foreword

$\mathcal{F}$ive years ago, a lot of people felt that I was a pretty good golfer. Even more thought that, because of my smooth tempo, my swing was technically sound. Unfortunately, however, I did not share their enthusiasm. In fact, the inadequacies I could feel in my action were making me distinctly unhappy. My shots lacked penetration, especially into any sort of wind; their parabolic shape and weak trajectory a product of my overly steep downswing arc. I was tired of improvising and compensating, tired of searching for new gimmicks to get me through another week.

Sure, I could have gone on being one of the best golfers in Europe, winning the occasional tournament and perhaps playing three and a half good rounds in a major championship – but that would never have been enough. I had, in fact, already achieved that. I was one of the best in Europe; I had won five tournaments on the way to topping the Order of Merit in 1983. I had contended in more than one major championship before falling away over the final nine holes. Enough for some people perhaps, but I was unfulfilled . . . and confused.

That, then, was the Nick Faldo who approached David Leadbetter at the end of 1984. Our first meeting was a brief one, David merely giving me some thoughts to work on. Six months of struggling later, however, I asked him to completely overhaul my swing. He did. My setup, takeaway, swing plane, leg action and balance all came in for criticism. And that was only the beginning. It took two years to fully construct the athletic swing I have today. It was a long two years, but I trusted David totally and stuck at it. Slowly but surely I started to see improvements in my shot making. I had a new concept of the golf swing. And as my confidence grew, my swing became more natural and less mechanical. The hard work had paid off. I became a

7

better player, a player I could never have been without the teaching methods of David Leadbetter.

It goes without saying that David is, I feel, the best coach in the game. He has great qualities, but his greatest asset is an uncanny ability to identify the root cause of a problem and immediately diagnose the proper cure. That invariably means working through one or more of his innumerable drills. They convey more than any words the feel of an athletic swing.

That word 'feel' is important. David is not a teacher of pure mechanics. He knows the difference between performing well on the practice range and on the course itself. There is thus no danger of him tying you in theoretical knots. What this book will give you is the chance to find out, as I have, just how good you really are.

Nick Faldo

Introduction

'DEVELOP YOUR OWN
ATHLETIC SWING AND
DISCOVER THE FORMULA
FOR GREAT BALL-STRIKING.'

Introduction

I have spent a large percentage of my life standing on practice tees watching golfers search for a swing they can repeat. Many of the motions I see are combinations of years of neglect, jumbled tips, clichés and, ultimately, confusion. Instead of having a solid foundation on which to build, these are people who early on developed bad habits in their swings and now spend most of their time trying to shore up the cracks. They move from one cliché to the next in the hope that 'it' will be the key to great golf. You know the kind of thing: 'stay behind it', 'drive your legs', 'extension', 'shift your weight' and all the rest. Although there is some truth in each, long-term improvement is forsaken in favour of 'quick-fix' solutions which are rarely effective for more than a few rounds.

It has long been my opinion that, despite the ever increasing numbers of people playing golf and the continuing improvement in equipment and course conditioning, the general level of play is staying pretty much the same. That can only be because too many players are seeking a shortcut to a better swing when, I'm afraid, there isn't one. So, assuming you have adequate physical ability, my message is this: apply yourself, and all you need in order to improve are the correct tools.

This book will give you those tools. It will guide you through the athletic swing stage by stage, conceptually and visually. You will build an athletic swing that is flowing, simple and repetitive. That, in turn, will bring the reward you seek – better golf.

I hear this from all my new pupils: 'I want to hit the ball consistently.' As far as the full swing is concerned, that means controlling the flight pattern of the ball, its trajectory, the amount of spin or curve, and the distance it travels. A simple task? No. Such are the complexities of the game that even the greatest players find it difficult to maintain consistency.

Imagine this. To win a tournament, you need a par on the last hole. After a good tee shot you are 175 yards from the putting surface. The ideal approach is a slight fade to a narrow green, guarded by bunkers to the left and right. You select, say, a 5-iron. Sounds tricky, but not impossible, right?

But look at it this way. With a hitting area on the clubface of 2.5 inches, you have to strike a ball only 1.68 inches in diameter. The 14.25-ounce club, which builds up a dynamic pulling weight of approximately 100 pounds during your 1.5 seconds motion, has to be swung at a speed approaching 90 miles per hour through an arc of approximately 18 feet. The ball is on the clubface for just 0.00035 of a second and to be hit the desired distance in the right direction it has to be launched at an angle of 42 degrees.

Now you can see why consistency might be a problem for even the most talented players! And when you add wind, the quality of the lie and the human element – your level of confidence – to the equation, it is amazing how precise your swing has to be. So no matter how hard you work on your technique, you can never be totally consistent. But you can get close. Using an athletic swing that is free of wasted motion or unnecessary compensations, you can maximize the efficiency of your ball striking. Not only will the number of good shots you hit increase, but your poor shots will be less penalizing. Imagine how exhilarating golf would be if you could stand behind your ball, picture its flight, trust your swing and execute the shot just as you imagined. The athletic swing will give you that ability.

Inconsistent ball striking or flight pattern can invariably be traced to overuse of your hands through impact. This stems from your body being out of position and your hands having to assume the role of leaders rather than followers. The more athletic a swing you create, the more chance you have of maximizing the speed and squareness of the clubhead as it strikes the ball towards your intended target. To accomplish this, it is my opinion that **both the direction and speed of the clubhead are controlled by your torso**. Your hands and arms remain passive – think 'active body, passive hands'. When the large muscles of your body control the smaller muscles in your hands and arms – I liken it to the dog wagging the tail rather than the tail wagging the dog – greater consistency is the result. That is the gist of the athletic swing: **correct linkage of the various components of your body with your hands, arms and club produces a dynamic motion**.

A word of advice on how to get the most from this book. First, read it from cover to cover. That will give you a feel for all that is involved in the athletic swing. Once you have that, it is time to start building. As with a new house, start with the foundations and work up. The book is designed to make you your own best teacher. Besides the written word, there are illustrations and exercises to foster the proper feel of the athletic swing. The text is divided into four chapters: *Preparation*, *The Pivot*, *Positioning* and *Linking it all Together*. Each stage leads into the next. Work at your own pace; don't try to build too quickly. Be patient with yourself. Only move on to the next stage when you feel you have mastered the previous one.

Nothing in the first three chapters requires you to actually hit a ball. Your mind is left free to concentrate on the mechanics of the athletic swing. A mirror or video camera are useful aids. Either will help you in two specific ways: (1) to check your position at any given moment; and (2) to add visual recognition to the important, but not completely reliable, 'feel' aspect of the swing. A few minutes' practice each day will soon see you well on your way.

Chapter four, *Linking it all Together*, is full of images and feelings – athletic keys – that allow you to work on your swing while practising or playing. The surest route to success is by way of these keys. They allow you to feel the parts and motions of the athletic swing. In effect, they focus your mind and allow your swing to work without you being bogged down by too much theory.

Your final goal is to convert your athletic swing to pure instinct rather than conscious thought. Then you will be able to concentrate not on mechanics but on playing the game. Remember that 'par to win' I mentioned earlier? Nick Faldo was in just such a situation on the 72nd hole of the 1987 Open at Muirfield. All the work, drills and thousands of balls Nick hit in order to perfect his athletic swing came down to one 5-iron approach. Even under the severest pressure, he was able to execute the shot successfully. Two putts later he was a champion and I know, at your own level, the athletic swing can make you one too.

David Leadbetter

1

Preparation

'AN ATHLETIC SETUP
CREATES THE CORRECT
STARTING LINK
BETWEEN YOUR BODY
AND THE CLUB.'

Preparation

Preparation is a combination of three important elements: the way in which you position your hands on the club (grip); the way in which you position your body in relation to the ball and club (stance and posture); and the way in which you position your body and club in relation to the target (alignment). They are all equally vital and done correctly they give you the best possible chance of success.

Indeed, what invariably distinguishes a good player from a poor one is their respective address positions or setups. You do not often see a good player with a poor setup or a poor player with a good setup. **A good player appears dynamic, athletic, relaxed and ready to move.** In contrast, a poor player often looks sloppy, non-athletic, tense and fidgety.

I cannot stress this strongly enough. **A good setup is the most important fundamental in every athletic swing.** Even a slight variation can ruin your chances of hitting good shots. What the address is designed to do is place the various components of your body in a balanced state with the club prior to setting them in motion. **Any swinging motion requires good balance.**

There is no question that even the best players work harder on their setups than on any other aspect of the swing. They know that **the surest route to consistency is through a disciplined preparation.** Such discipline is important. It is the finest attribute you can have when it comes to addressing the ball.

Use a mirror to assist you. Seeing, as well as feeling, particular positions is reassuring. Then you are free to make a good swing and concentrate on the target.

Work on your grip, stance, posture and alignment for a few minutes each day and your address will, in time, become as natural as breathing. It takes patience, but the rewards are great. And the beauty of it is, the setup is one area of the game where there are no

16

problems or stresses caused by actually having to hit the ball. Anyone can have an athletic setup. There are no excuses. Sure, we all have different body types, but the fact remains that the same preparation is applicable to all – tall or short, heavy or thin.

Let's look at each aspect in turn.

▬ THE GRIP ▬

A good grip may not lead necessarily to a good swing, but a bad grip is much more likely to cause a bad swing. Many golfers struggle all their lives with grips which can never encourage good moves in the swing itself. A good solid hold on the club is the first step towards correct positioning of the clubhead throughout the swing. After all, your hands are the only parts of the anatomy in contact with the club.

To fully understand what a good grip looks like, it is necessary to take it apart, piece by piece. Too often I see players with grips which may appear satisfactory on the surface, but which on closer inspection turn out to be one of the main causes of their golfing woes.

Generally speaking, a poor grip will put too much emphasis on your hands. That leads to them over-controlling the club and moving it out of position. **In an athletic swing, the role of the hands is reduced as much as possible**. Think of them as conductors through which the speed and power created by the turning motion of your body is transferred to the clubhead.

The statement that 'great players have great hands' really dates back to the days of the hickory shaft. Because of the flex and torque in those old shafts, the hands controlled the swing and squared the clubface. In the modern athletic swing your hands must act passively and simply respond to the motion of your body. To that end, I place great importance in positioning them correctly on the club in what I term a 'neutral position'.

That is not to say that good play is not possible with a less than orthodox hold on the club. There are certainly some top players who use what might be considered technically incorrect grips. But these players, through talent, superior hand–eye coordination and much practice, are able to compensate for their grips.

In fact, it is easier to adopt a neutral grip. It requires no compensations later in your swing and simply links your hands to the club.

17

The more neutral your hands are at address, the more neutral they will be at impact. Translated, that means you are less likely to manipulate the clubhead with your hands. It is not a rolling of your hands, but the turning motion of your body which squares the clubhead through impact.

Do not confuse this near elimination of hand action with that of wrist action. **The passiveness of your hands in the athletic swing does not mean that you swing stiff-wristedly**. On the contrary, the hingeing and unhingeing of your wrists is vital for transmitting power through the lever action your golf swing creates with your arms and club. And the way in which your hands are placed on the club influences this important wrist movement. If the club is held too much in your palms, the resulting lack of mobility will restrict the correct hingeing or cocking of your wrists. Conversely, a club held too much in your fingers will tend to make your wrists over-active and loose.

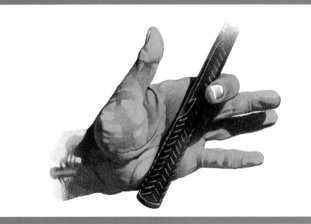

In a neutral grip, the club is held mainly in the palm of the left hand. It should run diagonally across from the pad at the base of the palm to the index finger.

Take a step-by-step approach to constructing a neutral grip. Start with your left hand; place it correctly, and only then bring in your right hand. That will ensure neither is in a more powerful position. They must work together rather than in opposition – **your grip is a two-handed alliance, not a battle for supremacy**.

In a neutral grip, your left hand holds the club primarily, though not exclusively, in the palm. The grip of the club runs diagonally across your hand from under the meaty pad at the base of your palm through your index finger. This gives a healthy balance between fingers and palm. As your hand is set on the club, the index finger creates a slight trigger effect. The small ridge created between the trigger and the second finger allows the little finger of your right hand to fit snugly between them.

When your left hand closes over the club, your thumb should be placed pretty much directly on top of the shaft. Looking down, you should be able to see the top two knuckles on the back of your hand. The 'V', or the line formed between the first knuckle on the index finger and the thumb, should point at your right ear.

So that your left hand sits naturally on the club, a slight angle must also be created at the back of your left wrist – exactly as if your left arm is hanging by your side (referred to as the 'dish angle'). Creating an unnatural flat or straight left wrist at address, where no angle is present, can impede your ability to hinge your wrists. Within that prerequisite, grip a little more firmly along the base of your last three fingers. Your hand must be secure, particularly at the top of the backswing and at impact where your grip is most susceptible to

The completed left hand grip has the thumb positioned on top of the shaft.

loosening. A snug fit between the meaty part of your palm and the last three fingers gives your left hand a secure hold on the shaft. Your grip must be comfortably firm rather than tight. This allows your left hand to 'accept' the hit as the club moves through the ball.

Note too, that the pad of your left hand does not protrude over the end of the shaft. At least the grip cap should be showing. This is important. While it may not contribute actively to better swings or shots, it does help maintain control. The left hand position is so important because, to a large extent, it is a reflection of your clubface. Where it points or faces at impact dictates the angle of the clubface and, in turn, the direction and flight of the shot.

In contrast with the left hand, the right holds the club almost exclusively in the fingers. The shaft should sit along the base of the fingers on a slight diagonal.

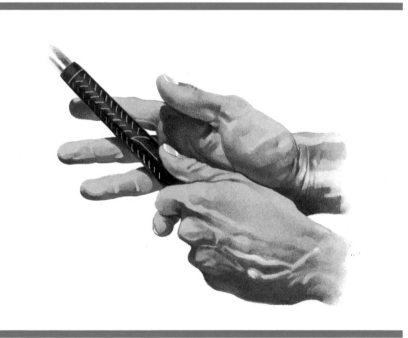

When you have your left hand positioned correctly, it is time for your right hand to join it on the club. But take care. If you are right-handed, naturally stronger on that side, watch for a tendency for your right hand to grab hold of the grip and try to dominate your left. It is vital that your hands work together as a single unit. **Linking your hands correctly on the grip is the first step towards your attaining the proper positions throughout your swing.**

There are three ways in which your right hand can join your left on the club. It can:

When gripping the club, extra pressure should be felt:
(a) in the last three fingers of the left hand;
(b) in the trigger finger of the right hand, and
(c) in the lifeline of the right hand on top of the left thumb.

- overlap (the Vardon grip), your right pinkie nestling in the ridge between the index and second fingers of your left hand;
- interlock, the pinkie lying between the first two fingers of your left hand;
- or it can simply lie below the left in what is known as the ten-finger grip.

I feel that the overlapping grip used by the majority of top players is best. It promotes the best feel while at the same time keeping both hands linked together. In it, **your right hand holds the club primarily in the fingers**. The shaft runs across the base of your fingers on a slight diagonal. When your hand wraps around the club, your left thumb fits snugly into the gap between the two meaty parts at the base of the palm on your right hand – almost exactly in the middle of your palm along the lifeline. Your right index finger sits slightly down the shaft to form a little trigger, your thumb adjacent to it on

When both hands are comfortably fitted on the club, the angles formed at the back of each wrist are virtually symmetrical.

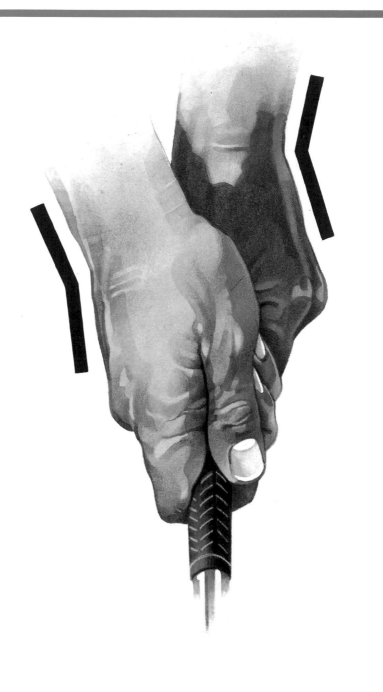

the left side of the grip. The 'V' between your thumb and forefinger points at your chin. Your right hand should be fitted snugly up the shaft towards your left hand so that they become a unit. And as with your left wrist, to ensure a neutral grip a slight angle is again formed at the back of your right wrist. Thus, both wrists are in fairly symmetrical positions.

The pressure points on your right hand, as with your left, promote a firm but not rigid hold on the club. **The lifeline on the palm of your right hand should push down on your left thumb.** There should also be a little awareness, or pinching sensation, in your trigger finger as it pushes onto the shaft. Be sure that there is an equal balance of pressure in both hands.

With both hands on the club, you should maintain a firm hold but feel particular pressure in the last three fingers of your left hand, in the trigger finger of your right hand, and in the middle of the grip with the lifeline of your right hand pushing down onto your left thumb. The pressure exerted by your hands should not be excessive. One sharp tug on the clubhead should be enough to loosen your grip, but not enough to pull the club from your hands.

It is easier to check on the correctness of the grip if the club is held up at angle of 45 degrees.

A little advice when working on your grip: it is easier to assume the correct position of your hands if you hold the club up in front of you at an angle of 45 degrees to the vertical. By having it so, your left hand can be positioned exactly, the shaft running across your hand diagonally. I see many poor grips where the hands are placed on the club while the shaft is angled downward. Gripping out in front also enables you to make sure that the leading edge of the club is vertical, and therefore square when placed behind the ball.

Practise taking your grip, even while watching television, for anything up to 20 minutes per day. Repeat until it becomes something you do without thinking. It may not be the most interesting of exercises, but correct positioning of your hands is too important to neglect.

■ THE SETUP ■

*N*ow that you have placed your hands comfortably and correctly on the club, you must properly position your body in relation to the ball. Your body must be placed in such a way as to encourage good balance during the swing. **Good balance is common to all good swings.** Without it, you are prone to make any number of bad shots.

Although the golf club is a relatively light object, it is, in effect, going to weigh an awful lot more when it is moving at high speed during the swing. Your body has to be in the position from which the swinging of this increasingly heavy object can be done freely, without hindrance.

In many cases I see, poor positioning of the body at address condemns a swing to failure before it starts. You need dynamic balance – balance that will allow the shifting of weight freely from almost a centrepoint, back to your right side and then through to your left side. To do that **you must set good body angles at address**. By maintaining these angles, the free, swinging motion you want will be that much easier to produce.

Let's start from the ground up.

There is a certain amount of feel and experimentation involved in setting the width of stance best for you. But there are two basic rules to follow:

1. your stance should be wide enough to promote stability and narrow enough to promote good motion;
2. the shorter the club, the narrower your stance.

However, the most important aspects are comfort, balance and a sense of liveliness in your feet and legs. Generally, this is best

24

The ball should be positioned opposite the left armpit for every club in the bag,
no matter the width of stance.What does vary slightly is the distribution of weight.

achieved from a stance in which **the distance between your heels is never more than the width of your shoulders.**

To allow your body enough room to pivot freely both back and through, your feet should be turned out at the same angle, somewhere between 25 and 30 degrees. Turning out your right foot encourages your right side to turn out of the way on the backswing. Conversely, turning out your left foot encourages the proper rotation of your hips through impact. Some players prefer to place the right foot at right angles to the target line, but I feel that can lead to overly restricting the turn of the trunk.

To accommodate the pivot motion, turn the feet outwards at an angle of about 30 degrees.

The position of the ball within the stance is something golfers have debated since the game began. The solution, however, is simple: **the ball remains in the same position – opposite your left armpit – for every club in the bag, no matter the width of your stance.** This maintains a constant relationship between the ball and your left foot.

If you do wish to vary the width of your stance, simply move your right foot closer to your left. The more lofted the club, the more you should draw your right foot in. In this way, the ball appears farther back in your stance, but, in reality, the relationship between it and your left side remains unchanged. For every club, **your left arm and the shaft should appear to form almost a straight line.** This represents the 'radius' of your swing and must be maintained, or felt to be maintained, throughout.

By adjusting the position of your right foot, and therefore the width of your stance, you are able to hit the ball at different points on your arc. Ideally, that means a slightly ascending blow with a driver all the way through to a descending blow with a short iron. This is important. There is a tendency in many players whereby their clubhead approaches the ball on the same overly steep angle both with irons and woods. Invariably this leads to poor divot patterns and inconsistent ball trajectory.

I like to see the clubhead **approach the ball on a fairly shallow angle with every club**. This leads to a much shallower divot pattern with the irons and, in turn, greater control. A more penetrating trajectory is obtained with the woods and that, of course, means more distance.

You have probably heard the statement 'create a flat spot at the bottom of your swing'. Well, a ball positioned opposite your left armpit will help create just that. Your club will be travelling fairly level to the ground through impact – not down and up sharply. This leads to a squarer, more solid hit. Adopting this standard ball position has another benefit too: the number of variables in your setup is reduced – perfect when consistency is your aim.

Only when playing a special type of shot should you move the ball from your left armpit checkpoint. For example, a low punch shot into the wind requires that you move the ball back in your stance. On the other hand, you can take better advantage of a wind-assisted tee shot with the ball a little farther forward.

Generally, when you are swinging well, you will 'find' the ideal ball position anyway. This is true in as much as when you are swinging badly, your ball placement tends to be out of position to suit a clubhead approaching on a poor path and angle.

Working hand in hand with ball position is the distribution of your weight at address (see page 25). For a driver, because you want to promote a slightly ascending blow, sweeping the ball away, place more weight back on your right foot than your left. Around 55 per cent right and 45 left is a good ratio. A mid-iron needs a slightly more descending blow, so a 50–50 distribution is more appropriate there. And a short iron, where your swing is naturally more upright, requires you to have a little more weight left than right in order to squeeze the ball off the turf. Around 45 per cent right and 55 left is pretty good.

Moving up from the ground, our next stop is the knees and, specifically, the amount of flex they should display.

Good knee flex has the value of lowering your centre of gravity. This aids balance and stabilizes your torso as it rotates to the right and left. **What you must create is a 'ready' position**. To encourage this, flex your knees only enough that, when you look down, vertical lines down through your kneecaps would carry on into the balls of your feet. That way, only around half of each foot is visible. If you

When the knees are properly flexed, the kneecaps are directly above the balls of the feet.

can see only your toes then your knees are flexed too much; all of your feet in view means that your legs are too straight. Make sure too, that your knees are spread a little apart. This will give you a slightly bow-legged appearance, better for creating the weight distribution necessary to keep your legs 'soft' and alive.

Now that you are in a 'ready' position with your feet and legs, **your hips should be set so that there is a slight upward tilt towards the target**. In other words, your left hip should be fractionally higher than your right. This puts the right side of your body in a lower, more passive position. Do not bother with any thoughts of lowering your right shoulder or raising your left – that can lead to them being set closed (aligned to the right). Combined with the fact that your right hand is set lower on the club than your left, placing your left hip in this position sets your right shoulder lower automatically.

Probably the most important angle created at address is that formed between your upper body and lower body. Bend from your hips. And do not confuse hips with waist. Bending from your waist tends to put your upper body too far over the ball, so bend from your hips. This angle is crucial. **The forward tilt of your upper body determines the way in which your spine moves in your swing**

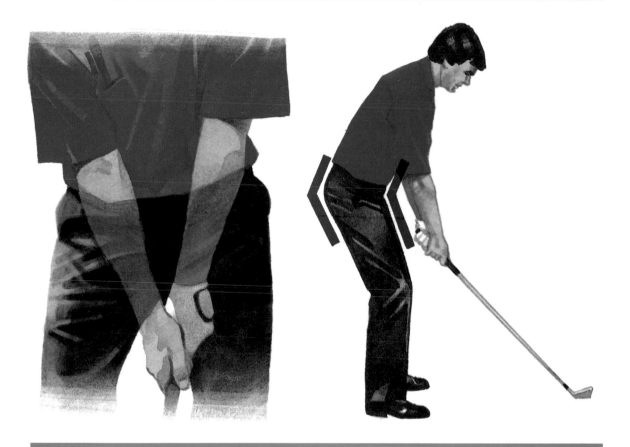

and, in turn, creates the axis that forms the plane on which you will swing the club.

Because we are placing so much emphasis on how your body is going to work in the swing, it is imperative that this position is correct. A poor spine angle will cause your hands and arms to be more active than need be. Remember: it is the turning, rotary motion of your body, not your hands and arms, which controls the athletic golf swing.

When the bend from your hips is correct, your buttocks will protrude slightly. Your lower back will be fairly straight; your upper back a little rounded. Your head should be angled so that your chin is both pointed to the right and 'up' enough that your shoulders can turn freely under it. These positions help relax your upper torso and

Left: At address, the left hip should be a little higher than the right. This automatically lowers the right side of the body. Right: The correct spine angle forms the axis of your swing plane.

29

place it in what I call a 'sit-tall' position. This encourages an even distribution of weight between your toes and heels. In fact, **there should be a feeling of weight hanging directly beneath you**. Weight concentrated too far forward or back can cause a loss of balance and poor motion. So stay centred and 'ready', your weight mostly on the balls of your feet.

Put yourself through this little test. At address, can you rock from heel to toe and back again? If so, your weight is correctly distributed. If you can only move your toes, however, then too much weight is on your heels. The reverse is also true. If you can only lift your heels, your weight is too far forward on your toes.

Look at it this way: a vertical line descending through the middle of your right shoulder or tricep should pass through your kneecap into the ball of your foot. This line is the balance point of your swing, around which you want to rotate. If the line is out in front of your knees, then your weight is too far forward. If the line falls behind your knees, your weight is too far back. By keeping the balance point constant, you are able to move at speed while still maintaining the body angles you set up at address. That is the secret – **keeping the body angles constant**.

A vertical line descending through the middle of your right shoulder or tricep should pass through the kneecap into the ball of the foot.

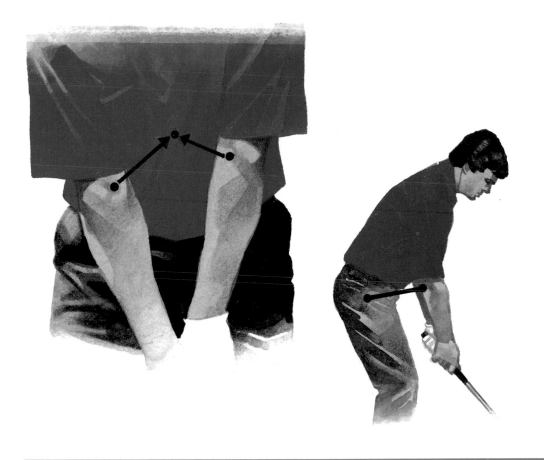

You should now be in position to place the club behind the ball. As this happens, allow your hands and arms to hang freely from your shoulders. Your arms must hang in such a way that they are turned outwardly upward. In other words, lines drawn from your elbow joints outward will intersect in front of your body (lines drawn inward will point at your hip joints). This triangle formed by your arms and chest should be roughly maintained as your arms and torso turn together into the backswing.

Your hands should be set low enough that an angle is formed at the base of your left thumb between the shaft and your left arm. As you will see later, this aids your first move into the backswing and reduces tension. You should feel some pressure under your armpits, between your upper arm and chest. If you cannot feel this, your arms

Left: *In any good address position the arms hang freely so that lines drawn from the elbow joints intersect in front of the body.*
Right: *The elbows should point directly at the hips.*

31

Above and right: *Get into the 'ready' position you require at address by means of this simple, four-step exercise:*
(a) standing upright, hold a club out in front of you;
(b) flex your knees until, looking down, you can see only half of your feet;
(c) drop your arms without bending forward, and
(d) bend from your hips and stick your buttocks out slightly. When the club touches the ground, you will be in the perfect position from which to begin your athletic swing.

are out of position. Pressure felt on your chest, down towards your elbows, indicates that your arms are too close to your torso. When they are too far away there is, of course, no pressure whatsoever.

That is a lot of information to take in about the setup, but I cannot overemphasize its importance. Now that you have the concept, the whole process can be simplified into this one little exercise.

From an upright start, hold a club straight out in front of you. Flex your knees until, looking down, your kneecaps are directly above the balls of your feet. At this point, most of your weight should be concentrated on your heels. Allow your arms to drop without any bending forward of your body, lowering of your head or arching of your wrists. The club should be hanging comfortably a few inches off the ground. Now tilt forward from your hips, lower your chin and stick your buttocks out until the clubhead rests on the ground. Your weight should now have moved forward onto the balls of your feet. For this setup to work effectively it is absolutely essential that it is relatively tension free.

So now you have the perfect 'ready' address position. Well-balanced and relaxed, this dynamic position is the ideal launching pad for the athletic swing.

■ ALIGNMENT ■

*A*s it inevitably involves a lot of feel, alignment in golf is very difficult. Without realizing it, you can get badly misaligned. It can vary from day to day, even shot to shot. It really is far more difficult than, say, shooting a rifle where you are standing and aiming directly at the target. When the ball is off to the side and you are forced to look at the target almost out of one eye, it's a difficult task. You are not looking directly down the ball–target line; you are looking to the left of that line. That gives you a distorted view, so lining up square becomes even more important.

Generally, it is true to say too, that the worse one is swinging then the worse one's alignment is. Alignment, as with ball position, very often tends to compensate for the way in which the club is being swung. For example, a player swinging too much from in-to-out instinctively places the ball back in the stance to accommodate his or her swingpath – one fault leads to another.

The only way to ensure a proper aim is by aligning your body around the position of the clubface. Work around it. Assuming the leading edge of the clubface is at 90 degrees to the target line, allow everything else to simply follow its lead. I advocate aligning your feet, knees and hips parallel to the target line (I am assuming the shot required is a straight one – hitting an intentional fade or draw may need some adjustment). **In contrast, your shoulders should, in my opinion, be a touch open (aligned left) with your right arm set slightly higher than your left.** There are two reasons

The feet, knees and hips are parallel to the line going through the clubface and ball to the target. The shoulders must be a little open at address. Thus, the right arm is set higher than the left.

for this open shoulder position: firstly, this is pretty much the position they will fill at impact, as you will see as we progress through the book. Due to the club being squared off not by the rolling of right hand over left, but rather the turning, rotary motion of your body, your shoulders will be open as your club makes contact with the ball. Secondly, it helps your unit of club, hands, arms and chest work away from the ball together. Take care not to overdo this aspect of the setup though. Your right arm should never get so far over your left that you are forced to move the club away on a severe outside path. Just be sure that only the lowest part of your left forearm is visible beneath your right arm when viewed from down the line.

This slightly open shoulder alignment is in sharp contrast to the positions I see many golfers taking up at address. Because they are so intent on getting the club approaching the ball from the inside, they set up with the right shoulder much lower than the left. That translates into a cramped position at impact and more hand activity than necessary.

A point golfers often miss is making sure that their eyes are aligned correctly. If your eyeline is not parallel to the line on which the ball must start, then it is easy to get a distorted view of the target. That, in turn, starts off your swing on the wrong path. **Make sure that your head, although tilted slightly to the right, allows your eyes to be parallel to the target line**.

To summarize, at address align your lower body – feet, knees and hips – parallel to your clubface–ball–target line. Your shoulders vary from this. They point just to the left of the target. While tilting your head a little to the right, allow your eyes to look down a line parallel to that of your lower body, i.e. parallel to the target line.

This is an old trick, but in my experience nothing better has come along to beat it.

Lay a club on the ground pointing straight out from the ball to the target (see page 35). Place another on the far side of the ball, parallel to the first. Then lay a third club along the line of your toes, again parallel to the others. That way, when the middle club is removed, there is no doubt that the remaining two are aligned parallel to your ball–target line. Now simply place your clubface at right angles to the target line. Align your lower body parallel to the club closest to you. No matter what your eyes say, trust it – you are lined up square. Adopt this procedure regularly to ensure that this important basic is not overlooked.

The completed address position shown face on and down the line.

*The completed address position
shown from behind and from the target.*

The purpose of correct preparation is to set off a chain reaction of good positions and motion through the swing. If you are wrong at the start, then the chain reaction activated is going to require you to manipulate the club or your body in order to get back on track. I cannot stress strongly enough the importance of monitoring your setup. It is the key link in building your athletic golf swing.

2

The Pivot

'A CORRECT PIVOT MOTION

IS THE LIFE BLOOD

OF ANY ATHLETIC SWING.'

The Pivot

$\mathcal{L}$earning the pivot motion of the body is the next step towards building an athletic golf swing. Now that a solid foundation has been built around the body angles described in the previous chapter, motion – in the shape of the proper turning, rotary motion of your body – must be introduced. Without making a good pivot you can never fully control the swinging motion of the club.

What is a pivot?

The dictionary defines a pivot as 'movement around a fixed point'. That is a fair description of the athletic swing except that, as we shall discuss, the transfer of your weight from its original static position at address to your right side and back to your left side is around two axis points rather than one. But more on that in a while.

What the pivot does

Your pivot motion provides three vital ingredients in your athletic swing:

(1) a coiling and stretching effect where your torso is wound up and loaded like a spring ready to unwind;
(2) a transfer of your body weight from one side to the other;
(3) consistent tempo or speed.

That, in a nutshell, is what your pivot motion is all about. A clear concept of how and what your body does will put you well on your way to becoming an athletic swinger.

For now, understanding the pivot action does not require you to use a club, not in the conventional sense anyway. You will need one only when working through some of the drills. This chapter describes the movement of your body – nothing more. **You must know what your body does during your swing before learning the roles played by your arms, hands and club.** Indeed, it is my experience that most golfers feel the benefits of a proper pivot more quickly when the club and perhaps more importantly, the ball, are removed from the equation. Let me give you an example.

A few years ago I was giving a lesson to a middle-aged gentleman of fair athletic ability. His friend, Fred, had come along to watch. My student had played golf for a few years, taken lessons from many different teachers and tried every tip he had ever read on the swing. As a result, some of the positions he adopted would have done credit to a contortionist. He did not, to say the least, have the most elegant of swings!

Anyway, after an exasperating session, I called on Fred to assist me. At first, he wasn't very keen. He had never played golf before, had no knowledge of the game or its technique and had, he said, only watched a bit on television. 'Perfect!' I exclaimed. 'You are just what I am looking for.'

After setting Fred up in a good posture (which took him only a little time to get right), I was able to get him to understand how his body was supposed to move. I told him how his lower body works in relation to his upper body, how the maintenance of his original body angles is important, how the athletic swing is a combination of resistance and freedom and how his weight moves from one side of his body to the other. Within a short space of time, this person with no pre-conceived notions was able to produce a good-looking motion.

The point of this exercise, as I explained to my increasingly incredulous student, was that until he had a grasp of what his body does during his swing his shots would never produce a repeating flight pattern.

Youngsters who start the game at an early age learn by imitation. Give them the opportunity to see some good, athletic swings and it is likely that their body motions will be fairly athletic in turn. However, it is my contention that most golfers never totally understand what constitutes a correct body pivot. As a result, they play all their lives with swings requiring constant patching, giving no thought to its inner workings.

But back to Fred. If he continued to repeat the posture and motion I gave him, he would, once they became instinctive, be ready to learn a good grip and then blend in a good arm and hand motion while imagining the track that the club follows. In other words, Fred would develop an athletic swing based around the principles of a sound posture and an awareness of how his body should move.

■ CENTRIFUGAL FORCE ■

*N*ow for a little physics lesson. The term 'centrifugal force' is used increasingly by teachers when disussing the golf swing. But I have found that only a few golfers really know either what it means, or what it does.

It is a force created away from the centre of your swing. Transmitting from your body, out through your arms and hands, it creates leverage, width of arc and clubhead lag. In turn, they create clubhead speed and maintain the club on a steady orbit or arc.

So how do we harness this important force found in the swings of all good ball-strikers? Simply, **it is the efficient coiling and uncoiling of your torso in a rotary or circular motion which maximizes centrifugal force**. Think of it this way: holding a piece of string with a weight on the end, begin to spin your wrist in an anti-clockwise direction. As long as your arm stays steady, the weight moves into a constant orbit. The quicker you spin your wrist, the faster the weight moves. The weight, though, will always be moving much faster·than your wrist – the centrifugal force created will see to that.

Centrifugal force keeps a spinning weight in a constant orbit.

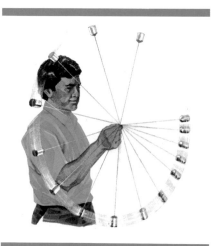

This centrifugal force or outward pulling of the string is maintained by the movement of your wrist. It is that which keeps the weight in orbit. If your wrist moves out of its original position, the weight moves out of orbit. Your golf swing displays identical characteristics. If your body does not move correctly, the club will not move on the correct plane or orbit. It will also lose speed. That means shots lacking in both distance and direction.

In the same way, the relationship between body and club during the golf swing is very much like a pair of ice skaters. I'm sure you've seen this on television; the lead skater (representing the body in the golf swing) is the hub around which his partner rotates. He revolves quite slowly while the female skater (representing the clubhead) is moving at a tremendous speed. This is a perfect example of how centrifugal force can be built up around a relatively slow moving axis and transferred to another, much faster object. Remember: the dog must wag the tail.

The lead skater rotates slowly and as a result of centrifugal force his partner rotates much more quickly.

Your golf swing starts from the address position where the club is virtually static. It then gathers speed as it changes direction and culminates in a whip-like action through the ball. This acceleration stems from the turning or pivotal motion of your torso – the power base or engine room of every athletic swing. That is how centrifugal force is maximized. Through the motion of your body, power is built up; power that flows through your arms and hands into the clubhead. The impression that the power in your golf swing stems

Any athletic swing, like throwing a discus, involves the build-up of power through the coiling motion of the body.

from the motion of your hands and arms is a false one. Just like a discus thrower who builds up power through the coiling motion of his or her body, you use your hands and arms merely as conductors of your torso-created power.

That is not to say your hands and arms play no part in your golf swing. They most certainly do. Even the most efficient pivot motion could not generate a great deal of clubhead speed operating alone. But there is a definite chain of command – your hands and arms must react to, not dominate, the movement of your body.

It should be clear to you that maximizing the centrifugal force in the clubhead requires a certain amount of physical ability. That is why it is very difficult to play golf well with a bad back. A lack of mobility or flexibility in your back reduces the rotary motion of your spine and cuts the supply of power to your arms, hands and club. When forced to take over the task of moving the clubhead, they are less effective.

As proof of how important your body motion is, try hitting some balls while sitting on a stool, your feet off the ground. To hit the ball any distance is all but impossible because the only source of power is the swinging motion of your arms. Remember: **the power base in every athletic golf swing is the turning motion of your body – your pivot.**

As you work on your pivot motion, realize that you do not rotate around only one fixed axis point, your head. Imagine a line drawn down the inside of your right shoulder, through your right hip joint and past the inner part of your right thigh into the ground. Now imagine the same line travelling down the left side of your body.

The pivot in the athletic swing involves not one but two axis points.

Rotating around each axis point creates a 'turning weight transfer'.

These are the two axis points around which every athletic swinger rotates, back and through.

Rotating around your right axis point, then your left, will encourage what I call a 'turning weight transfer' in both directions. Your body weight, from a fairly even start at address, moves to your right heel on your backswing and toward your left heel on your downswing. It is quite normal for your head, especially on the backswing, to move a little laterally as you turn. It should certainly be free to swivel. Keeping your head overly still can only restrict your motion around your two axis points.

An incorrect rotation around your two axis points can, in fact, lead to a so-called 'reverse pivot'. This occurs when, on your backswing, your weight does not move around your right axis point, but hangs on your left side. On the downswing, that translates to your weight

The normally disastrous 'reverse pivot' occurs when the weight remains on the left side on the backswing and shifts to the right coming through.

moving onto your right side instead of your left. By severely reducing the ability of your body to correctly control your hands and arms, this causes all manner of bad shots.

Although your pivot motion should not include any pauses or breaks in motion, I am, for the sake of clarity, going to split it here into three pieces:

(1) your backswing or pivot motion to the right;
(2) the transition from backswing to downswing as the body changes direction;
(3) your downswing or pivot motion to the left.

This, I feel, is the best way for you to attain a clear understanding of the complete motion.

━ BACKSWING ━

*A*dopt your address position in front of a mirror, then allow your club to drop to the floor. Maintaining your body angles (especially your shoulder tilt, left higher than right), place your right hand on your left shoulder and your left hand on your right shoulder. You are now in position to begin what I call the 'criss-cross' drill. It is designed to give you the feel of a proper pivot.

The starting point for the pivot action is the navel. Turn it gradually to your right and, in unison, allow your weight to initiate its shift by rocking onto your right heel. This results in a very subtle lateral move in your hips before they turn. A chain reaction now takes place. Your hips and shoulders start to rotate and your left

Left: *The 'criss-cross' drill is designed to give you the feel of the proper pivot motion of the body.*
Right: *The flex in your right knee must be maintained throughout the backswing. It creates the resistance necessary for a coiling motion.*

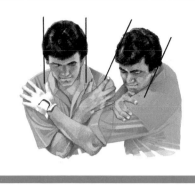

Allowing the head to swivel encourages the rotation of the body.

shoulder moves down and across slightly to ensure that your shoulders turn at right angles to the axis of your spine.

However, not every part of your body is moving. There must be some resistance down below so that your upper body produces as much windup or coil as possible. That resistance comes from your right knee. This is a key aspect of any dynamic swing: **the flex in your right knee must be maintained.** You should, in fact, have a sensation of 'sitting down' on it.

As the rotation of your hips and shoulders around your right axis point continues, the torque (twisting force) and stretch increases. You should feel a tightening sensation down the left side of your back. Your left knee is pulled inward slightly and your left hip and shoulder move in unison with their right counterparts. Your shoulders can now rotate freely around your head, perpendicular to your spine. As I have already stated: **do not make any attempt to keep your head absolutely still.** In fact, allow your head and neck to swivel slightly to the right to accommodate the rotation of your body.

You have reached the end of your backswing when these five things occur:

(1) your chest has turned until it is over your right leg;
(2) your left shoulder is under your chin;
(3) your upper back muscles are stretched and your whole back is facing the target;
(4) there is a tightness in the muscles of your right thigh as a result of the resistance in your right knee;
(5) your left knee points behind your imaginary ball while keeping quite a gap between itself and your right knee.

51

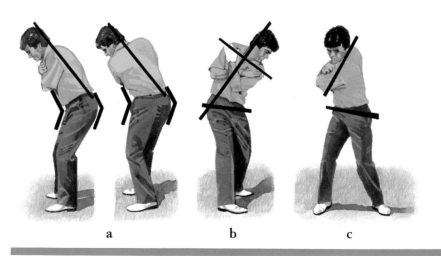

Above: *The completion of the pivot motion to the right from three angles.*

a   b   c

IMPORTANT POINTS TO NOTE
ABOUT YOUR BACKSWING PIVOT

- The spine angle you create at address is maintained so that there is no raising or lowering of your upper body.
- Your shoulder turn is perpendicular to your spine and your hips appear to have turned on a fairly level plane (your left hip will feel 'high').
- Your shoulders turn at least 90 degrees to the target; your hips turn approximately half that amount.
- A vertical line drawn up from your left hip would show that your left shoulder is turned well behind the line.
- A vertical line drawn down from your left hip would appear inside your left foot.
- Most of your body weight is on your right side before you change direction.
- Your left knee appears behind a line drawn across your toes running parallel to your ball-target line.
- As an aid to your body rotation, your right knee, although flexed, swivels slightly. For example, if at address your knee points straight out at 'twelve o'clock', at the 'top' it should have moved to 'one o'clock'.

Below, left and right:
(a) *The angle of the spine set up at address must be maintained during the backswing.*
(b) *Turn your shoulders on an angle perpendicular to your spine.*
(c) *Turn your shoulders at least 90 degrees, your hips about 45 degrees.*
(d) *Your left shoulder should be turned behind a line drawn up from your left hip.*
(e) *A line drawn down from your left hip will enter the ground just inside your left foot.*
(f) *At the 'top' most of your weight is on your right side.*
(g) *Your left knee does not shoot straight out – it should appear behind a line drawn across your toes.*
(h) *Your right knee, while maintaining its flex, should swivel slightly and point at 'one o'clock'.*

d   e   f   g   h

That final point raises a question. How high should your left heel rise? Well, that really depends on your level of flexibility. The more flexible you are, the more you will be able to keep your left heel down. Follow this basic rule: as long as your left heel rises only as a result of your pivot motion, any amount of lift is all right.

At first this winding-up motion will probably strain you a little as your muscles stretch. Don't worry, it will soon ease through practice. Although you are building up torsion, you do not require tension. **Keep your body as relaxed as possible.**

Practise your backswing pivot in front of a mirror. Do it slowly at first, feeling each part of your body and the roles they are playing. Repeat it often and soon your backswing will be an instinctive rather than a contrived move.

■ TRANSITION ■

*P*ossibly the most crucial stage **in any athletic swing is the change of direction when your club and body start back towards the target.** It is vital that the backswing and downswing are joined by a motion that is flowing and dynamic. How often have you seen someone make a nice smooth backswing then hit a poor shot through 'snatching' the club from the top back to the ball? The transition from back to forward swing must be smooth and unhurried.

In fact, for a fraction of a second, your body will be moving in two directions simultaneously. As your upper torso completes its winding up away from the target, your lower body is already starting to unwind towards the target. This vital move, particularly noticeable in long hitters, creates additional torque and leverage.

A smooth transition from backswing to downswing is dependent on the movement in your lower body, specifically your legs. They are the stabilizers in your athletic golf swing, providing balance and support as your upper body winds and unwinds.

As your upper body completes its backward motion, your forward motion is triggered by a movement from your left knee. It moves on a slight diagonal, towards the toes on your left foot. At the same time, your right knee holds. There must be no sliding of your legs towards the target. Your left knee, in fact, does not want to move beyond its original starting position. This separation of the knees gives your

Above: *The transition from backswing to downswing produces a separation of the knees and a squat, 'sitting-down' look in the lower body.*
Left: *During your transition your body moves in two directions at once. As your upper body completes the backswing, your lower body is already moving forward.*

legs a squat, rather 'sit down' look. To make this change of direction truly dynamic, the clockwise rotation followed by your right hip and buttock on the backswing should continue a little as your left knee moves forward and separates from the right.

At this point too, your weight remains predominantly on your right leg; your right heel is flat on the ground and your upper body is coiled to its maximum. The large muscles in your upper back are also fully stretched. This not only increases the torque of your swing, but also, as you will see, has an effect on your control of the club as it changes direction. In turn, that determines the plane on which the club will travel back to the ball.

This move is an inherent part of any athletic swing and needs a lot of practice to develop the proper sensations and feel. Here are two exercises I suggest you do:

1. Although the criss-cross drill you used for the backswing is equally applicable to this transition stage, even more emphasis can be placed on the production of torque if, instead of placing your hands on your shoulders, you hold a club behind your

Simulate the feel of your transition by placing a club behind your shoulders and making your pivot motion. You should feel pressure across your back as your legs move into their transition position.

shoulders. From there, make your backswing motion. As you turn your back on the target, move your lower body into the transition position. The shaft will cause increased pressure and resistance across your back. Note that your knees, hips and shoulders at this stage are pointed to the right of the target.

Start off slowly with this drill. A few repetitions are enough at first, so build up gradually. Before long you will have a real sense of power and balance as you ready yourself for the downswing.

2. Take your address. Holding a club by the head with your right hand, place it on top of your right thigh. Let it run diagonally down your groin until the grip is behind your left knee. Now make a normal turning motion with the right side of your body. While building up the pressure in your thigh, maintain the flex in your right knee with the shaft of the club and allow your left knee to 'separate'.

Hold this position for a few seconds. That sensation will give you an understanding of the holding pattern of the legs, so necessary as you start into the forward part of the swing.

You can understand better the role of the legs in the transition by placing a club on top of your right thigh and running it down behind your left knee. As the left knee moves, feel the pressure in your thigh as the right knee holds.

━ DOWNSWING ━

$\mathcal{T}$he role of your downswing is to release all the torque that has been built up and stored to this point. Once the transition has taken place, the most efficient way of achieving that is for your torso, after having moved a little laterally, to rotate around the left axis point.

Focus on the mid-section of your torso, from your sternum down to your crotch. With your legs resisting and acting as support, your mid-section (as with the discus thrower) must unleash itself. The energy created translates into tremendous clubhead speed.

But we are getting ahead of ourselves.

Once through the transition sequence, your left shoulder shifts away from your chin so that your body can move laterally a few inches, towards your left axis point. Once achieving this position, your sole thought should be to rotate your trunk to the target – the downswing can be described as a 'lateral rotary motion'.

As far as the shoulders are concerned, there is not an immediate drop of your right shoulder or raising of your left shoulder. In fact,

The discus thrower unleashes his stored-up energy through the rotation of his body.

your shoulders move on a fairly level plane prior to your right shoulder making a distinct downward movement and your left shoulder moving up and around. If your right shoulder does tilt too early, you will be unable to rotate to your left axis point.

Your left leg should firm up appreciably as it supports the unwinding of your torso around your left axis point (be sure to maintain a constant spine angle throughout this unwinding process). This rotation of your torso continues until your hips are fully turned, your chest facing the target and your right shoulder closer to the target than your left. That signals the completion of your clearing around your left axis point. Your weight has now shifted with your body rotation so that it is predominantly on your left side, feeling pressure mainly on your left heel. You will be standing fairly erect with a

Left: *As the downswing begins the shoulders move on a fairly level plane before the right shoulder drops and the left moves up and around.*
Right: *The finish position of the athletic swing, where the right shoulder finishes lower than the left.*

slight curve in your spine at the finish – be sure that your head is tilted slightly and your right shoulder is lower than your left.

This whole process is a matter of correct sequencing. What generally upsets the chain of events is overuse of the legs. Players either make an excessive lateral slide or turn out of the way too quickly. To avoid both, focus on keeping your right heel on the ground until it is pulled off by the unwinding of your torso.

Avoid any possibility of too much lateral sliding of the legs by focusing on your right heel. It should stay on the ground until pulled up by the unwinding of your torso.

IMPORTANT POINTS TO NOTE
ABOUT YOUR DOWNSWING PIVOT

- After your left shoulder moves away from your chin, both shoulders rotate and unwind on the same tilted angle as that of the backswing.
- As your body unwinds towards the target, your head tilts in the opposite direction. This helps maintain your spine angle and keeps your right shoulder working under your chin.
- As your body unwinds and your right knee drives inward, it works behind your toeline – not out towards the ball.
- Your spine angle is maintained well past your imaginary impact position. Only as you near the end of your swing should it change in order to release pressure on your back.
- At the completion of your motion five things have happened:
    (a) your right foot, although up on the toe, is aligned inward slightly;
    (b) your right knee is just behind your left;
    (c) your hips face slightly left of the target;
    (d) your right shoulder is closer to the target than your left;
    (e) your head will be forward of the position it occupied at address.

Because of the natural tendency in good players for the legs to get too far ahead or outpace the upper body, one of the feelings you want to promote is that **your upper body opens up your lower body to the target**. No doubt this is the opposite of everything you have ever read on the swing – that the lower body should always pull the arms and club through – but fear not. As long as you have achieved a proper transition, your legs will stabilize the whole unwinding process of your torso. This feeling will allow you to be perfectly balanced through the crucial area of your swing – impact.

(a) *Initially moving on a level plane your shoulders rotate on the same tilted angle they did on the backswing.*
(b) *A slight tilt of your head away from the target helps maintain your spine angle and keeps the right shoulder working under your chin.*
(c) *The angle of your spine is maintained well past impact.*
(d) *Your right knee works inwards and never crosses out beyond your toeline.*
(e) *Your body in the finished position.*

For good balance, maintain your finish position for a few seconds.

Once you have established some understanding and feel for the three aspects of the pivot – backswing, transition, downswing – simply put them together in one flowing movement from start to finish. This smooth motion is best described in the following two ways:

1. It is very much like a figure eight in the way that it moves. Your right hip turns behind you going back, your hips move slightly diagonally to the right of the target starting forward, then your left hip completes the figure eight by clearing behind you going through.

2. Picture yourself standing in a barrel with your right hip a couple of inches inside the rim and your left hip about 6 inches inside the opposite rim. This allows for the slight lateral move on the backswing before you rotate and the corresponding diagonal lateral move forward as the swing changes direction before it rotates back to the ball.

Think of your pivot motion with your hips as a figure eight.

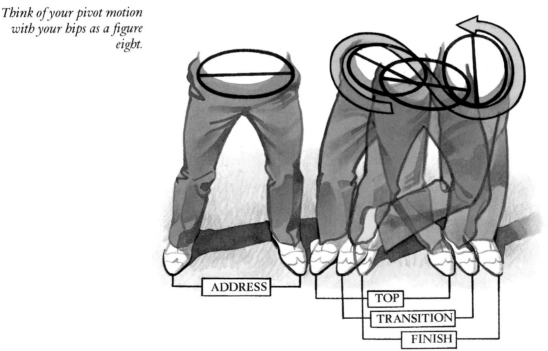

ADDRESS

TOP

TRANSITION

FINISH

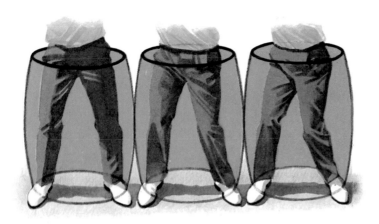

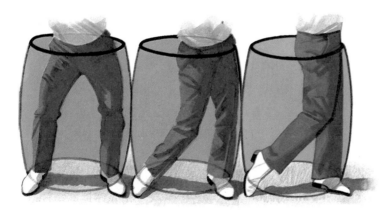

Picture your pivot motion as being within a barrel.

Although there is a lot of detail in this chapter, performing the drills regularly will quickly give you a feel for the power being built up, stored and released by your pivot. Alternate between the criss-cross and club-behind-the-back drills. They are best for fostering the feel of a proper pivot.

The complete pivot motion, emphasizing the mid-section of the torso, shown face on and down the line.

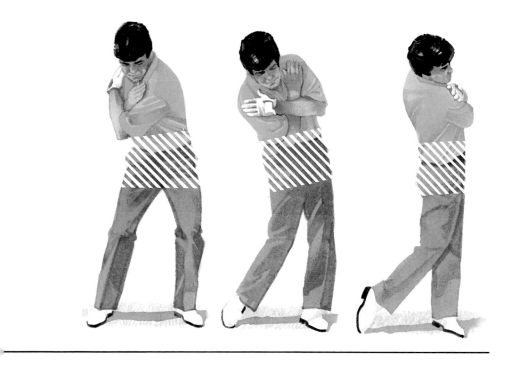

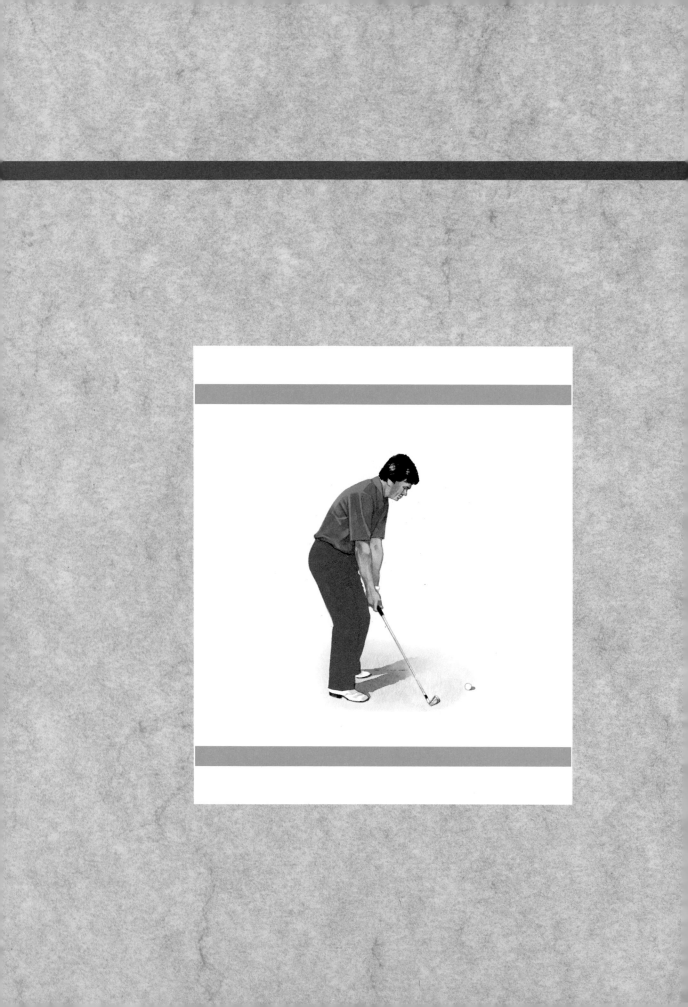

3

Positioning

'GOOD SWING MOTION
RESULTS FROM
A CHAIN REACTION
OF GOOD POSITIONS.'

Positioning

To create and maintain an athletic swing it is necessary to have an understanding of where the club is positioned in relation to the pivot of your body. So in this chapter, which I recommend you use primarily for reference, the swing is broken down into stages or links.

These links are a 'freeze-frame' version of an athletic swing. By being conscious of each one you will have a better understanding of where you should be during your swing. In turn, that will enable you to identify more easily where things go wrong.

However, be aware that these links are *within motion*. They merely represent points along the route followed by your athletic swing. What they give you is a clear picture of the roles played by your arms, wrists and club – *not* an action replay of the athletic swing itself. When your pivot is functioning correctly, your arms, wrists and club move in harmony with your body. Any independent movement not directly tied to your pivot is likely to lead to the breakdown of your dynamic motion.

I have boiled the athletic swing down into eleven links. Each one can only be as good as its predecessor. Thus, when analysing your action and looking at a problem, you have to be aware of the difference between cause and effect. Whenever I see an error in the swing of a pupil, I look back to address until I find where the problem originates. A mistake early on adversely affects what happens later.

Having a clear understanding of the early links in the swing is vital. One is able to consciously control these early links but, as the swing progresses, because of the speed of the motion, it becomes largely reactive and instinctive. Get the initial links correct in conjunction with the proper pivot, and the rest of the swing will simply be a chain reaction. Having said that, by having a total understanding of each link throughout the swing, it will allow you to have an awareness of the complete picture and what you are trying to achieve.

This chapter, then, has three main aims: to make clear the functions of your wrists and arms (I prefer to say wrists rather than hands – the proper hingeing action of your wrists is a vital part of your athletic swing); to make you aware of the plane and path on which the club swings; and to pinpoint the position and angle of the clubface during your motion. (In order to make the stages totally clear, I have re-emphasised some of the more vital body positions covered in the pivot chapter as they relate to each link.)

However, don't make the mistake of taking your eleven links onto the course with you. It is impossible to think of all eleven, then hit the ball at the same time. Work on this chapter while on the practice tee or, preferably before that, at home in front of a video camera or mirror. By placing the club in the correct position at each link, holding it for a few seconds, then moving on, you are able to familiarize yourself with your athletic swing. Look from face on and behind (down the line towards your target) when analysing your positions from address to just before impact. For impact and beyond, it is more useful to swing directly at the camera or mirror.

NOTE: As an added guide, I am including some of the common errors I have observed during the course of my teaching. These are bordered with red, as opposed to green, rules.

■ LINK 1 ■

𝒯he first link in your athletic swing is the address position described in chapter one. By now you should realize how important it is, so important that it requires constant checking. I'm going to mention some of the important points once again to refresh your memory. Remember: bad habits are as easy to ingrain as good ones and, without you realizing it, your setup can change.

The line you observe running parallel to the shaft of the club up through your body is termed the original shaft line plane. As you will see, this is an essential reference point and guide.

Left: *The athletic address position.*
Right: *Address, illustrating the vertical balance point line and the original shaft line plane.*

POINTS TO NOTE

- A vertical line descending through the middle of your right shoulder or tricep should pass through your kneecap into the ball of the foot.
- Your weight should be balanced on the balls of the feet.
- Pressure must be felt under the upper arms and onto the chest.
- At address, you have to feel relaxed but dynamically poised to move.
- Your feet, knees, hips and eyes are parallel to the target line, with the shoulders slightly open.

Common errors

1. A vertical line drawn from the middle of the right shoulder, appearing behind the knees, indicates the body weight is too far back towards the heels.
2. A vertical line drawn from the middle of the right shoulder, appearing in front of the knees, indicates the body weight is too far forward.

Common errors 1 and 2.

The first checkpoint of the backswing at 'eight o'clock', with the butt end of the club positioned opposite the middle of your right thigh.

■ LINK 2 ■

*I*magine this. At address, your body is positioned within an angled clock face, the ball representing six o'clock. **Your aim is to get your club, hands, arms and body moving in unison away from the ball until you reach your first checkpoint – when the clubhead points at 'eight o'clock' and the butt end of the club is opposite the middle of your right thigh.**

As the butt end moves, your navel must move with it. Your hands, in fact, move a short distance while the clubhead travels a lot farther. At this early stage, your hands are still passive, moving only in response to your body. Also, the pressure exerted by your left arm on your chest at address remains constant. This ensures that no separation occurs between your arms and body.

I like to think of this motion between links one and two as the 'moveaway' rather than takeaway. To me, takeaway conjures up a picture of hands and club moving before, instead of with, the body.

When viewed from behind, there is no daylight visible between the right and left arms.

POINTS TO NOTE

- The butt end of your club points at your navel.
- The gap between your body and the butt end of the club narrows from link one to link two.
- The angles formed during the address position at the back of your left wrist (the dish angle) and at the base of your left thumb are maintained.
- When viewing yourself from behind, looking down the target line, your right arm appears to be on top of your left. No daylight is visible between the two.
- Looking down at your eight o'clock position, the path taken by your hands is seen to be closer to your body than that taken by the clubhead. In other words, your hands are inside the clubhead. As a checkpoint, lay a club on the ground diagonally between the left heel and the toes of the right foot. The eight o'clock position can be seen when the shaft and the leading edge of your club appear parallel to the shaft on the ground.

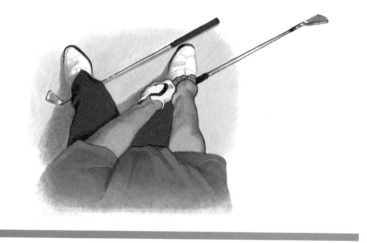

Laying a club on the ground between your feet serves as a checkpoint for the eight o'clock position.

■ *Common errors* ■

1. A swing, initiated by the hands and arms, which pushes the club away from the body. Result: a wide gap between the two and no turning of the navel.
2. A swing, initiated by the clubhead, causing a separation of the elbows and a rolling open of the clubface.

Common errors 1 and 2.

1   2

■ LINK 3 ■

*A*gain keeping your imaginary clockface in mind, your objective here is to get the clubface pointing at nine o'clock.

In order that your hand and arm action remain linked to your pivot, your hands should only travel a very short distance from their link position. There should be no conscious extension of your arms or widening of your swing radius. The club is carried to link three by your body pivot, together with a slight hingeing of your wrists, a gradual clockwise rotation of your left forearm and a subtle spreading of your elbows. This results in the clubface opening up. In effect, the stage has been set for the upward movement of the club *on plane.*

The club has now moved to 'nine o'clock' with the shaft parallel to the ground, ready to move upwards on plane.

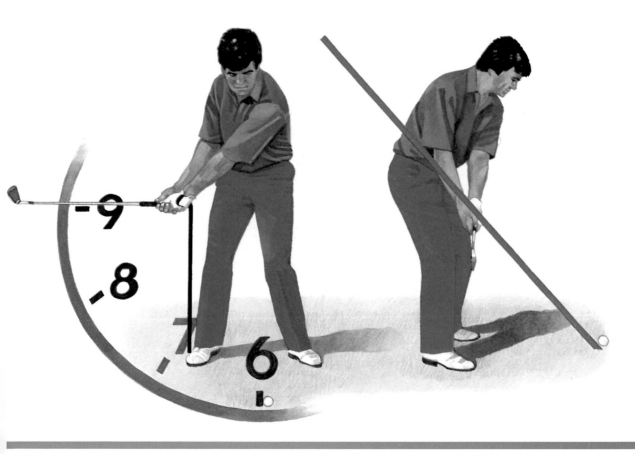

POINTS TO NOTE

- Your body, although beginning to rotate, has visibly turned only a little.
- A vertical line drawn from the butt end of your club would enter the ground just outside your right foot.
- Your left arm is tight to your chest and your right elbow is close to your right hip.
- The palm of your right hand faces the ball–target line in a 'shake hands' position.
- Wrinkles at the back of your right wrist are the first sign that the hingeing of your wrists is taking place.
- The shaft of the club is parallel to your toe line, parallel to the ground and intersects the original shaft line.
- The toe of the club points straight up towards the sky.

At nine o'clock the palm of your right hand is parallel to the ball–target line in an imaginary 'shake hands' position.

Common errors

1. Arms extended too far away from the body and no hingeing of the wrists.
2. An over-rotation of the left forearm, forcing the clubhead too far behind the hands into a position where the shaft is no longer parallel to the toe line.

1   2

Common errors 1 and 2.

■ LINK 4 ■

*B*etween links three and four your left arm moves up to a point where it is parallel to the ground. This is a particularly important checkpoint in as much that from here on, during your actual swing, the pivot of your body assumes almost total command of your arm and wrist action. Being correct up to this point allows the rest of the swing to be that much easier. Although you should continue to be aware of the action of your arms and wrists, there is no further need for you to consciously influence their movement. From link three, the upward motion of the club (the plane) is effected by the **turning of your body**, folding of your right elbow and natural hingeing of your wrists. Your right elbow, in fact, now works away from your body causing the arc of your swing to widen.

From its horizontal position at link three, **the shaft makes an upward shift and appears on a more vertical plane than that which it occupied at address**. It does not continue on a line parallel to the original although, as we shall see later, it does return to it. **Look at the plane as being bowed or warped rather than as a straight line**.

77

When the left arm is parallel to the ground, the wrists are fully hinged and the right arm appears above the left.

This upward bowing movement is a result of the correct hingeing of your wrists and working of your right arm. When viewed from face on, your right elbow, as it continues to separate from your left, appears higher than the left elbow. Two things remain unchanged: the attachment of your left arm to your chest and the dish angle at the base of your left wrist.

The shaft has now steepened away from the original shaft line plane.

POINTS TO NOTE

- Your body pivot is now approximately 75 per cent complete.
- Your left arm, while still linked to your chest, is angled away from the target line and points behind you.
- Your right arm appears above your left and the spreading of your elbows initiated at link two is complete.
- Your swing is at its widest point with your left arm extended but relaxed.
- Your wrists are fully cocked.
- The shaft, now more vertical than before, bisects your right bicep when viewed in a mirror.
- The angle of the clubface is parallel to the left forearm.

■■■ *Common errors* ■■■

1. A body rotation that is either (*a*) complete or, conversely, (*b*) less than 50 per cent.
2. A left arm that has worked away from the chest, rather than rotating across it, and points parallel to the target line rather than away from it.
3. A shaft plane that is either (*a*) too flat (laid off) or (*b*) too upright in relation to the right bicep. Too flat and it runs through the elbow joint when viewed in a mirror; too upright and it bisects the shoulder joint.

Common errors 1a, 1b, 2, 3a and 3b.

1a

1b

2

3a

3b

■ LINK 5 ■

*T*his position is commonly referred to as the 'top' of the backswing. Realize that this link is purely a reference point. In an actual swing, it is not a position that you swing to and stop at before starting down. No, it happens within motion. Some swings may appear to have a momentary pause, but this is only as a result of the body beginning its move in the opposite direction.

Left and right: *The 'top' of the backswing.*

The 'pre-set' drill.

Simply stated, link five is the fully set position reached at link four transferred to the 'top' by the completion of your pivot action. This transfer also applies to the pressure under your left arm. As your backswing completes, your left arm rides up your chest while continuing its attachment to it. Thus, the radius of your swing formed by your left arm and the club shaft is maintained.

The role played by your arms and wrists at this stage is minimal. They should feel totally passive. Any influence on the club is purely the result of swing momentum and the weight of the club. No conscious movement of your arms and hands is required.

If you have trouble attaining this position, try what I call the 'pre-set' drill. After adopting your normal setup, lift the club up directly in front of you until the shaft is at 90 degrees. Do not extend your arms away from your body. Observe the angles formed at the back of your wrists. Now, while maintaining those angles, simply turn your body and place the club at the top. This not only puts you in the perfect position, but conveys the feeling of passive arms and wrists you wish to encourage in your normal swing.

If the club is on plane (through the bicep) at link four, a correct pivot motion will ensure that it attains a perfect plane 'at the top'. Your right elbow supports your left arm and the club, and you are now ready for the change of direction.

POINTS TO NOTE

- Your left shoulder is under your chin and your back is facing the target.
- Your left arm remains linked to your chest and, though extended, stays relaxed.
- The gap between the upper and lower halves of your right arm should form the letter 'L' at your elbow. This maintains the radius of your swing.
- The inside portion of your right arm from wrist to elbow should parallel the angle of your spine.
- A shaft placed across your elbows would be parallel to the ground.
- Your left thumb is underneath the shaft, maintaining the dish angle at the back of your left wrist.
- Ideally, for a full swing with a long club, the shaft should be approximately parallel both to the ground and the target line. A swing short of parallel will result in the shaft pointing to the left of the target.
- The clubface hangs down in a square position, at an angle parallel to your left-arm plane.

Left: The upper and lower parts of your right arm should form a letter 'L' at the elbow.
Centre: The right forearm should be parallel to the angle of your spine.
Right: A shaft placed across your elbows should appear parallel to the ground.

▬ *Common errors* ▬

1. A less than 90-degree angle formed at the right elbow, causing a narrowing of the swing radius.
2. A separation of the left arm from the chest, and a raising of the right elbow, lifting the club out of its proper plane and aligning it right of the target.
3. A loss of the dish angle at the left wrist. Too convex or bowed (*a*) leads to the clubface pointing skyward in a 'shut' position; too concave or 'cupped' (*b*) results in the clubface hanging straight down in a very 'open' position.

Common errors 1, 2, 3a and 3b.

Up to this point the athletic swing has largely been controllable because of the relatively slow speed of your backswing. Coming down, however, as your motion accelerates it is largely reactive and cannot be controlled consciously. Remember: because centrifugal force plays such a large part in your downswing, you have to trust your instincts and feel. That, however, does not alter the fact that you need a clear concept of what the club is doing all through your athletic swing.

■ LINK 6 ■

*L*ink six is actually link five transferred down to a point where the left arm is again parallel to the ground. And this is where the difference between a good swing and a bad swing becomes apparent. In a good athletic swing, the change-over from backswing to downswing is all but invisible. In a poor motion the two directions of the swing remain distinctly separate.

The change of direction of the club is effected by the transition move described in the previous chapter. The steeper backward plane is replaced by a flatter downward plane, making the original shaft line a key reference point. **The downswing flattens until the club is parallel to, although slightly above and outside, the original line**. The slight outward motion of the hands and left arm, plus the flattening of the shaft, from link five, is perfectly natural and can be attributed to the dynamic motion of your body as it moves forward. It can be clearly seen when the swings of top players are viewed in slow motion.

Left: *The 'L' shape of the right arm is maintained during the initial stages of the downswing.*
Right: *The club has flattened onto a plane that is parallel to the original shaft line plane.*

Sense your wrists retaining, or even increasing, their hinge and really emphasize your left arm–chest pressure point at this stage. There must be no separation or independent arm action.

POINTS TO NOTE

- Your upper body feels closed (aimed to the right) in relation to the target.
- Your legs have assumed a 'sit-down' position.
- Even as your right elbow moves closer to your body, the 'L' shape of your arm is retained. This ensures that the radius of your swing remains constant.
- Both wrists remain fully hinged.
- The club is parallel to your original shaft-line plane. The butt end points at a spot outside the ball–target line.
- The clubface once again is parallel to the back of your left arm.

■■■ *Common errors* ■■■

1. An overly steep downward plane caused by a poor transition and the left arm and hands working too far away from the body.
2. The right arm jamming itself into the body, thereby narrowing the swing radius.

Common errors 1 and 2.

1   2

▬ LINK 7 ▬

*A*lthough when in motion it may appear a little different, this link is a virtual mirror image of link three, where the butt of the club is just behind your right leg. I call this the 'delivery' position; the clubhead ready to be delivered to the back of the ball.

From link six on, your right arm gradually straightens and your left arm begins to rotate downwards. Both arms should feel linked to your body. In order to retain the leverage you need to unleash the club through impact, your wrists have not begun to unhinge.

Left and right: *At the 'delivery' position, the shaft is parallel to the ground and the target line. Your wrists form a 90-degree angle with the shaft.*

POINTS TO NOTE

- Because most of your weight is still on the right side, your right foot remains fully on the ground.
- Your right elbow is just in front of your right hip.
- Your wrists form a 90-degree angle with the shaft.
- The shaft is parallel to both the ground and the target line.
- The toe of the club points vertically up towards the sky.

Common errors

1. The shaft coming from (*a*) too far inside (hook) or (*b*) outside (slice) the target line.
2. An early release of the wrist cock as a result of the right elbow being trapped behind the right hip.

Common errors 1a, 1b, and 2.

1a   1b   2

LINK 8

Impact. This is the culmination of all that has gone before it. The quality and direction of your shot is decided here. It is the most dynamic in a series of increasingly dynamic positions. And as such, you cannot simply place yourself at impact during motion if the previous links are not joined together in a dynamic fashion. What you can do, however, to assimilate this link,

The dynamic impact position.

Left and right:
Maintaining your spine angle through impact keeps the club 'planed'.

is pose at impact for a few seconds with the clubhead pressed firmly against a ball. This is one of the images we will discuss in the next chapter.

It is helpful to understand impact by being aware of its various aspects. That is why I am detailing every one so thoroughly. From link seven on, where the club is approaching the wall on a path inside the target line, there is a squaring and releasing of the clubhead by:

(a) the rotary action of your body;
(b) the rotation of your left forearm toward the target;
(c) the straightening of your right arm;
(d) the unhingeing of your wrists;
(e) the butt end of the club working left, in towards your body.

Our main goal is to achieve a situation where the plane of the shaft at impact and the original shaft line closely match one another. Thus, the club returns to the ball in the same position it filled at address. I term this 'getting the club "planed" through impact'. And the reward? Consistent ball striking, the aim of every golfer.

POINTS TO NOTE

- Your spine angle at impact is identical to the angle at which you set up at address.
- Your head and spine are behind the ball.
- Your hips are partially facing the target, up to about 45 degrees open; your shoulders appear more open than they were at address.
- Your right shoulder is tilted lower than the left and the top part of your left forearm is visible when viewed from down the line.
- Your left arm is tight against your chest, your right elbow linked closely to your right hip and your right arm almost fully extended. Your elbows are the same width apart as they were at address.
- The back of your left wrist is flat; the wrist itself raised a hair. The right wrist is angled (cupped) inward.
- Your left leg, though a little flexed, is firm and braced and provides resistance. Pressure is exerted on your left heel. Your body weight should feel fairly even.
- Your right knee points in, behind the toe line. Your right foot is rolled inward, up on the toes.
- The butt end of the club is forward of the clubhead, the grip pointing towards the inner part of your left thigh.
- The clubface appears slightly open to the target line. As the ball stays on the clubface for a fraction of a second, the face is actually square only when it leaves the club.

■ *Common errors* ■

1. A loss of spine angle as the head and tail bone move away from their original positions. The arms are no longer linked to the chest.
2. A slide of the lower body, placing the head too far behind the ball.
3. Shoulders turning on too steep an angle (*a*). The right tilts too far under the left, creating a big gap between both arms – thus the shoulders appear closed and the hips too open. This causes (*b*) too vertical a shaft plane and off-centre hits.
4. An early release of the club which allows the clubhead to pass the hands and 'cup' the left wrist.

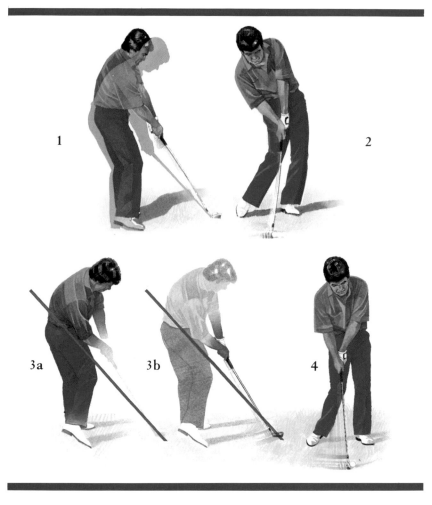

1
2

3a
3b
4

Common erors 1, 2, 3a, 3b and 4.

▬ LINK 9 ▬

*T*his post-impact position is a mirror image of link two, the eight o'clock position. While the butt end of the club continues to move left, the clubhead moves only a little way until it points to four o'clock. This is a clear indication that your hands are passive in the athletic swing. The turning of your body controls the release and squaring of the clubhead without any independent hand or arm action. **There is no need for any conscious crossing over of your hands, right over left, in order to square off the clubface.**

POINTS TO NOTE

- Your body continues to turn, but your head remains in its impact position.
- Your arms remain linked to your body. The upper part of your left arm hugs your chest, your right elbow adjacent to your right hip.
- The squared clubhead has moved past the hands and the butt end of the club points at your navel.
- As in link two, the path taken by the hands is closer to the body than that taken by the clubhead – the hands, once again, appear inside the clubhead.

▬▬ *Common errors* ▬▬

1. The head moving forward and past its impact position.
2. The left arm leaving the chest, holding the right arm too far underneath in a 'blocked' position and causing a hand crossover and premature closing of the clubhead.

Common errors 1 and 2.

1   2

▬ LINK 10 ▬

*W*hile your hands and arms are working to the left of the target, centrifugal force is hard at work. It creates a pulling force on your arms and clubface which straightens and extends your arms away from your body for a fraction of a second. Be aware of this as you work towards this next checkpoint.

At link four your left arm was parallel to the ground, your wrists fully hinged. Here, however, in order to obtain the same relative wrist position your right arm has to move just beyond horizontal. Because of centrifugal force, your wrists have not fully re-hinged at the point where your right arm is parallel to the ground.

Left: *At this stage your body rotation is almost complete and the wrists are fully hinged.*
Right: *The shaft appears parallel to the original shaft line plane.*

POINTS TO NOTE

- Your body is almost fully rotated, facing the target, the majority of your weight supported by your left leg.
- Your head, although in the position it filled at impact, swivels to allow your eyes to look 'under' the shot.
- Your right arm is fully extended exerting pressure on your chest.
- Your left elbow is folded downward.
- The backs of both your wrists appear slightly 'cupped'.
- As in link six, the shaft should be parallel to and above the original shaft-line plane.

▬ *Common errors* ▬

1. A conscious effort to 'stay behind the shot', leading to the body hanging back and the right hand appearing too much on top of the left.
2. A conscious effort to over-extend the arms towards the target.

Common errors 1 and 2.

1   2

▬ LINK 11 ▬

*Y*our finish position is purely an extension of link ten. Your arms are simply carried forward by the completion of your pivot. What link eleven does give is some insight into the quality of the previous ten links. It is rather like tasting a cake mix. You can tell right away what ingredients need to be added or subtracted in order to produce the correct blend. The end of your follow-through should depict balance and linkage (how the arm swing has blended with the pivot). A sure test is to see if you can hold your finish for a few seconds. If you can, it shows that your body has supported and controlled the accelerated release of the club.

Left and right: *The finish position.*

POINTS TO NOTE

- The right side of your body is closer to the target, your head forward of its starting position.
- The pressure you felt on your chest under your right arm at link ten is still present.
- Your elbows are approximately the same width apart they were at the 'top' of your swing.
- Your left elbow is away from your side supporting the club and your right arm is extended across your chest.
- The slight 'cup' position at the back of your wrists, seen in link ten, is maintained. Your left thumb is directly under the shaft.
- The shaft appears across the back of your head at an angle slightly below the horizontal.

■■■ *Common errors* ■■■

1. An incomplete rotation of the body towards the target.
2. Arms too high, the club hanging almost vertically (normally a result of trying to keep the club 'on line').

Common errors 1 and 2.

1   2

As I said in the introduction to this book, the main aim of any athletic swing is to get the dog to wag the tail – the body to control the arms. This is most noticeable from link four onward. So spend a lot of your practice time getting your first four links correct.

Keep referring to this chapter. In order to maintain a steady rate of improvement it is helpful to see your actual swing on a slow motion video-tape. Then you can compare each link of your swing to the illustrations here. Take care when filming yourself, however. The positioning of the video camera is vital. If it is set up at an oblique angle you will get a distorted picture. Be sure it is directly opposite you, at right angles, when viewing from face on. Equally, when the camera is to your right, looking at the target (down the line), it should be aligned parallel to, and halfway between, your toeline and ball–target line.

To further assist your video analysis, get yourself a washable felt-tipped pen so that you can mark different angles on the television screen. For example, when viewing down the line you can draw lines on either side of your body to indicate your spine angle and trace the shaft of the club at address to respresent the original shaft line plane.

A video camera is a useful tool when analysing your swing.

I also recommend you outline your head in order to check its movement. By following these guidelines, you will soon see any change in your body angles and observe clearly your shaft plane lines. This type of analysis really quickens your learning process. When working on your static positions, practise in front of your mirror. Hold each position for a few seconds until your are familiar with it, then move on to the next one. Do them slowly and stay relaxed. There is no hurry. Regular sessions will help your feel and imagery – it is a good idea at times to practise each link while gripping down on the club. By focusing your attention on the butt end, this will increase your awareness of the plane of the club and its position all through your swing. Alternatively, practising with your eyes closed brings each link more sharply into your mind's eye.

Once you have a clear picture of all eleven links, you are ready to join them into one flowing motion.

4

Linking it all Together

'RELATING FEELINGS
AND IMAGES TO
MECHANICS CREATES
A SIMPLE, INSTINCTIVE
GOLF SWING.'

Linking it all Together

*S*o far, your athletic swing has not been a swing at all. Everything you have studied – the preparation, pivot and positioning – has been in parts and, as such, consciously controllable. Now it is time to link all the components together into an instinctive swing motion. Anyway, I'm sure you are anxious by this stage to see the benefits of your change in technique when actually striking a ball.

Before attempting to hit balls though, there is one more step you need to take. I suggest you make many complete slow-motion swings – without a ball and without pausing at any of the links. Make some swings with your eyes closed, in order to feel the eleven links learnt in the previous chapter being joined together into a whole swing. Build up the speed of your swing as your confidence increases. As you learn the athletic swing – then put the ball in the way – you will achieve the ultimate: no conscious hit at the ball, merely a swing through it.

A smooth blending of its pieces (rhythm) in sequence (timing) at a good speed (tempo) is what typifies an athletic golf swing. To achieve all three your whole action has to be totally instinctive. This is done through creating images (pictures) and feelings (sensations) in your mind. I call these images and feelings 'athletic keys'. You could say that they form the link between physical know-how and mental application. There is no question that these keys, as opposed to conscious thoughts, are the finishing touches you need to take your mechanically sound swing out onto the course.

It is true to say also that there is a certain amount of trial and error involved in finding the right image or feeling. However, by having a few to choose from, you have the opportunity to experiment and find the ones that work for you. Every top player uses athletic keys when practising and playing. They change them periodically, too. And this is fine as long as the keys relate to the basic structure of the athletic swing.

I have listed the athletic keys in the sequence in which I feel you should try them. The order is linked to the learning process you have already gone through in chapters one, two and three, even if some keys overlap. At the end of each key there is a descriptive phrase. Use them as cues. They are designed to trigger responses from your subconscious.

A word of caution: do not focus on more than one key at a time. Too many can be distracting, create tension and inhibit the natural, freewheeling motion you require. Focusing on one key keeps your mind clear and your body relaxed.

■ ATHLETIC KEY 1 ■
'Getting the swing primed for action'

A common tendency I see in many players is an overly tense setup position. The stationary ball seems to have a hypnotic effect, inducing stiffness and tension where there should be relaxation and readiness. As a result, these players start their swings with their small muscles (hands and arms), rather than their large ones (body).

To get your big muscles into action and start your swing smoothly, your body and arms need to be relaxed so that they can link together with the club. Stay in constant motion. For example, a gentle rocking action from heel to heel keeps your legs active and free from tension.

So that you can properly sense the clubhead in your hands, and to keep your upper body relaxed, a waggle can be helpful. It also aids you in picturing and feeling the type of shot you want to play. Waggle the club gently two or three times by allowing your left hand to make a short clockwise rotation. The butt end of the club should actually move towards the target while the clubhead shifts back about a foot. Note too, that although there is a slight wrist movement involved in the waggle, it must be smooth and controlled, not quick or 'handsy'.

After a momentary pause to get your body settled, the best way to get the club into motion is a 'kick-start' from your right knee towards

103

A waggle helps you feel the clubhead.

the target, in conjunction with a slight leftward (no more than a couple of inches) rotation of your hips. Then, as your hips and navel move to the right they pull the club back. Practise this pre-shot routine until it is an integral part of each swing. Done smoothly, it is the initiator of good tempo in every athletic swing.

CUE: 'Kick and go'

The right knee 'kick starts' the swing into motion.

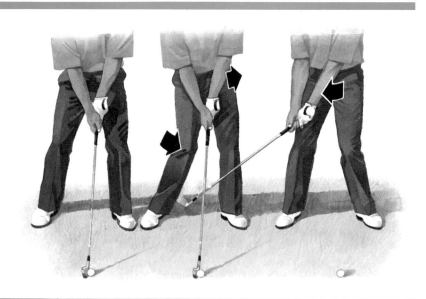

104

■ ATHLETIC KEY 2 ■

Keep the navel–club
relationship constant

$\mathcal{E}$stablishing a link between your body and club early on in your athletic swing is essential. Focus on your navel. Although it is not strictly true to say that the butt end of the club points directly at your navel at address, it is close enough to use as a reference point.

Adopting your normal posture, place the butt end of the club in your navel. Choke down on the shaft so that your arms are extended; maintain your spine angle; move your navel and the club to eight o'clock. Then, to visualize the position of your club and body just past impact, move the club forward to four o'clock.

Remember this drill when you come to grip the club normally and make a full swing.

CUE: 'Navel and club together'

The 'club in the navel' drill.

■ ATHLETIC KEY 3 ■
The club stays under the shelf

*V*isualize a shelf running above the club at address, parallel to the ground and extending from the eight o'clock position to four o'clock. Initiate your swing by feeling that the butt end of the club moves away low. This will keep your hands working underneath the shelf. Not only does this foster the proper linkage between body and club, it also helps maintain both your centre of gravity and spine angle.

Try to reproduce this powerful feeling coming into impact, at impact and past impact – in other words, between eight and four o'clock.

CUE: 'Butt end low'

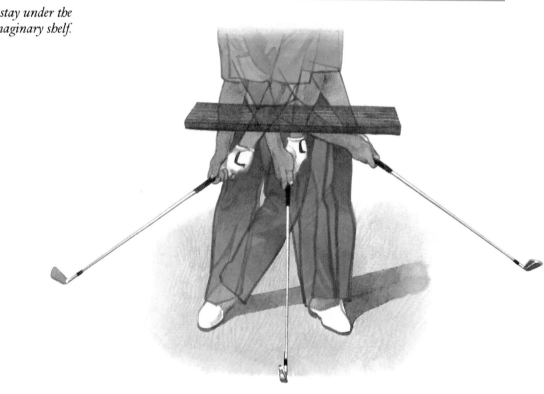

The hands stay under the imaginary shelf.

■■ ATHLETIC KEY 4 ■■
*Big muscles control
small muscles*

$\mathcal{T}$he quality of any golf swing is normally determined in the early stages. The period from address to link four, where the left arm is parallel to the ground, is vital in every athletic swing. Most errors are committed here; and inevitably they cause problems later on.

When working on building your swing, move the club to link four, check your position, then hit shots starting from there. Any arm and wrist action is basically over, so all that is required is that you complete your pivot motion back and through.

To promote a rhythmic beginning to your swing, gently pump the club a couple of times, moving your arms and body in unison. Then

Complete your backswing after 'pumping' the club.

complete your backswing and swing through. Feel how the release of the club through impact is controlled by your body rather than your hands.

CUE: 'Pump-1, pump-2, and go'

■■ ATHLETIC KEY 5 ■■
*Light-feeling club means
right technique*

On making a correct swing, not only should you be in balance but so should the club. If your wrists set the club correctly from eight o'clock there is a certain lightness and quickness attached to it, as if the clubhead was missing. When the club is out of position – out of balance – it feels heavy and more effort is required to make a swing.

CUE: 'Eight o'clock and weightless'

*The club should feel light
at 'eight o'clock'.*

■■■ ATHLETIC KEY 6 ■■■
Mirror-imaging the swing

On many respects the athletic swing mirror-images itself; especially in the way in which
(a) the body turns back and through;
(b) the wrists hinge up, hinge down and rehinge up again;
(c) the shaft at impact all but retraces the original shaft line plane at address.

Develop this mirror-image feel by starting your swing at link ten – 'left'. From there, turn your body to the 'right', allowing your arms and club to swing through link four to the 'top' in the normal manner. Then swing through to the finish 'left', passing through links six and ten on the way.

This exercise, as well as encouraging the mirror image aspect of your swing, also gets things flowing together from the start.

CUE: 'Left, right, left'

Picture the swing as a mirror image, back and through.

▬ ATHLETIC KEY 7 ▬
The change in swing plane

*A*s I have said, the plane of your athletic swing goes from a slightly steeper angle on the backswing to a shallower one on the downswing. When working on your plane, relate to the butt end of your club. During your backswing, the club initially moves back on the original shaft line and then shifts upward. Visualize the butt end making a 'C'-shaped move as it works inward and upward in a slight concave manner. As your body changes direction, your shaft plane flattens onto a line parallel to and slightly above the original shaft line.

CUE: 'Steepen, then flatten'

Left: *Imagine the butt end of the club making a 'C'-shaped move to the 'top'.* Right: *The change in swing plane from backswing to downswing.*

■ ATHLETIC KEY 8 ■

*Getting loaded into the right side
at the 'top' of the swing*

$\mathcal{I}$t is essential that your body 'loads up' onto your right side on the backswing, ready to spring into action on the downswing. To attain this loaded, coiled position, your big back muscles have to wind up and stretch against the resistance of your right knee. It is very much like an archer pulling the bowstring taut in order to propel the arrow a vast distance.

To get loaded correctly, your spine has to turn behind the ball. This may feel as if you are moving 'off' the ball somewhat with your body, but it is simply your spine rotating and shifting to your right axis point.

Assist this winding-up process by allowing your head to swivel. In fact, with longer clubs, where your swing is wider, even allow it to move a fraction to the right. What feels like a big move 'off' the ball will, in all probability, be minimal when you check it in a mirror or on your video.

CUES: **'Move off it'**
'Get behind it'
'Stretch'
'Load up'

Like the archer, get the feeling of loading up at the 'top' of the swing.

ATHLETIC KEY 8A

A more consistent position at the 'top'

*A*lthough there should be no stop at the 'top' of your athletic swing, it is sometimes a good sensation to feel. Imagine that you are swinging the clubhead, your hands, arms and club into the same 'slot'. By doing so your backswing will be that much more consistent in terms of plane, width, length and pace.

This is true of every club, despite the fact that a driver and wedge attain slightly different positions at the 'top'. When you reach your slot, the rest of your swing will react and happen naturally.

CUE: 'Into the slot'

Swing the club 'into the slot'.

ATHLETIC KEY 9

Your body moves in two directions at once

*O*n any dynamic motion – for example, throwing a ball or serving in tennis – the body at one point is moving in two directions. In your athletic golf swing this happens in your transition, between winding up on the backswing and springing forward going down. Do not think of starting everything back down together. As your upper body, hands and arms complete the backswing, your left shoulder under your chin, your lower body is actually moving forward.

Feel your transition by making swings with the club held off the ground.

This strong athletic move can best be felt when swinging the club out in front of you, a few inches above the ground. Make your swinging motion on this fairly horizontal plane, allowing your body to rotate and wind to the right. As you are completing your backswing, start your left knee towards the target. Your legs will take on a squat 'sit-down' look as your body continues to unwind and the club releases to the finish.

This is the most powerful move in the athletic swing. It creates a situation where the clubhead lags behind the hands, which in turn leads to tremendous clubhead speed as the lagging head catches up to the hands through the impact area.

This exercise also encourages a good rotary motion and accentuates the flatness of your plane coming down.

CUE: 'Wind up – left knee'

■ ATHLETIC KEY 10 ■
Returning to impact

$\mathcal{T}$his tell-tale position is a direct result of all that preceded it. Even so, it is a real advantage to have a pure image and feel for what should be happening at impact. An open body position at impact is an integral part of any athletic swing.

With your hands ahead of the clubhead, it should feel as if you are covering the ball with your body and 'trapping' it with the head of the club.

This impact drill will increase your awareness. After addressing the ball, make a slow swing, returning the club and your body to the perfect impact position as seen in link eight. Pose it for a few seconds, as if pushing into the wall, noting the pressure on the inside of your braced left leg. Now, starting from this pose swing back and

At impact, feel as if you are hitting into a wall.

through. Sense that you're tracing over your ideal impact position as you strike the ball and swing through to the finish.

CUES: 'Trap it'
'Cover it'
'Into the wall'
'Hit into your left side'

■■ ATHLETIC KEY 11 ■■
Turn your chest towards the target

*Y*our legs must support the rotation of your trunk away from and towards the target. By working the lower body correctly, this will allow you to use your upper body aggressively as you rotate through the ball. The transition move initially places your body in a slightly closed position. From that point on, as you approach the ball, your chest should start to open up gradually towards the target. If there was a soccer ball suspended in front of you, it would be as if you were 'chesting' the ball.

Do not confuse this with being 'over the top', a term used to indicate that the upper body has started outward as the downswing

Imagine chesting a suspended soccer ball as you rotate towards the target.

begins, throwing the club steeply out of plane. Invariably, slicers fall into just such a trap.

Remember: a good transition sets the trend for an inside the line approach into the ball.

CUE: 'Chest to the target'

■■ ATHLETIC KEY 12 ■■
The golf swing is a two-sided move

A question I am often asked is whether golf is a left- or right-sided game. It is neither. It is two-sided: both have parts to play at different stages of the athletic swing.

To begin the swing, your left shoulder pushes down, back and across. The right half of your body, as your wrists hinge, then completes the pivot motion back. To initiate the downswing, your left knee moves towards the target. Halfway down, as in throwing a ball, your right arm and shoulder chase down the target line ensuring that

Swing the club with your right hand only to emphasize the right-side release.

the clubhead accelerates and stays square through impact. This chain reaction culminates in your right side releasing the club to the finish. Emphasize this right-side hit by swinging a club with your right hand only. Once you have the feel, you can even hit some balls one-handed.

As you can see then, the swing can be summed up as 'left–right, left–right', with more emphasis on the right in the hitting area.

CUE: 'Hit it with the right side'

■ ATHLETIC KEY 13 ■
Keep the clubface square

*K*eeping your hands quiet through impact helps maintain a square clubface at the point of contact and for a few inches past it. This allows your body to control the release of the club. Avoid any early rotation of the right forearm over the left and premature closing or toe-up position of the clubface.

Hitting shots using a split-hand grip helps maintain a square clubface.

Although consciously controlling the club through impact is all but impossible, the 'split hands' drill can help you get the feeling of passive hands. Grip an eight-iron with your hands an inch or two apart. Hit some shots. It will prove difficult at first, especially if you previously owned a swing that relied upon excessive hand action through impact. Soon though, your shots should start to fly straight. Focus on these three feelings:

(1) the clubface staying open longer and pointing upward towards the sky;
(2) your right hand staying 'under' your left – the back of your left hand and the palm of your right hand partially facing the sky;
(3) the butt of the club working left – the path of your hands staying inside that of the clubhead.

Right to the end of your athletic swing, there should be no cross-over of your arms. The follow-through is simply an upward hingeing motion of your wrists.

CUE: 'Right palm faces the sky'

▬ ATHLETIC KEY 14 ▬
Linking your arm swing to your body motion

*A*t address, your left and right elbows should be looking at their corresponding hip joints. In the crucial areas back of the ball, at the ball and just past the ball, this elbow–hip relationship should be maintained. This ensures that

Linking the elbows and hips together.

your arm swing is linked to your body turn and that one does not outpace the other. Hitting little wedge shots helps to foster this feel and makes certain that the tempo of your swing is controlled by the pivot action of your body.

CUE: 'Elbows to hips'

■ ATHLETIC KEY 15 ■
The athletic swing consists of two turns

𝓡educing the whole athletic swing to its simplest form – turning the body away from the target, turning the body through to the target – is your final goal. Although, as you will realize by now, there is considerably more than just a

The ultimate swing cue: turn and turn.

turning motion in your athletic swing – for example, some lateral motion, maintenance of spine angle, wrist hingeing and shaft plane. Focus on your big muscles working the swing. You must achieve a situation where you have no thought of your arms, hands or club coming into play. That is the true sensation of the dog wagging the tail.

CUE: 'Turn and turn'

These feelings and images will assist you in transferring the mechanics of the athletic swing into your subconscious. Some of them will be good for you, but some won't. Certain keys may feel good one day, but be elusive the next. Great players normally have a few keys on which they can fall back. So, although you should never be afraid to experiment, only work on one at a time. Go in with an open mind. Believe me, hitting upon the key that will allow you to strike the ball solidly is a lot of fun.

HOW TO PRACTISE YOUR
■ ATHLETIC SWING ■

*B*e realistic. When you are making swing changes, expect some bad shots. Don't panic, especially in the early stages of building your athletic swing. Remember: you first have to work on a technique – the results come later. Do not fall into the trap of thinking that a good shot means a good swing or that a bad shot necessarily means you made a bad swing.

Don't stand on the range hitting ball after ball. Make a lot of practice swings. Work with a relatively easy club at first; a 7-iron, say. Then, as you gain confidence, change your club often enough that you gain the same feel with each one in the bag. Always aim at a target, placing your two clubs on the ground, and change that target every few shots. Make use of the drills in this book to break up your practice time. In fact, I recommend that you never hit more than 30–40 balls in an hour on the range.

Work systematically with a purpose in mind. Start with your setup; move to your pivot; then your positioning. Use an athletic key every time you hit a shot. Sense the swing rather than think it. But remember: get into the habit of periodically using a video camera or mirror to help you monitor your progress.

Make sure you also take time to develop your own pre-shot routine while on the practice tee. Watch the top players; they all have a rhythm and pace to their routines. That means picking a target, lining up with that target from behind the ball, walking up to the shot, settling into your setup, waggling, 'cueing' and swinging.

And the end result? Greater consistency in your shot pattern. Very little side spin should be produced. The squarer-faced contact resulting from your more efficient swing means the ball will travel in a fairly straight line. You may, of course, pull or push the occasional shot, but rarely will you hook or slice, the ball curving excessively in flight. If anything, however, your shots should fall slightly from right-to-left. This is due to the fact that the club approaches the ball from inside the target line.

The improved angle on which your club approaches the ball will produce shallow divots with your irons and a more penetrating ball trajectory. This makes the ball more likely to stay on line and less vulnerable to strong winds. The involvement of your big muscles in your swing motion will maximize your clubhead speed and, in turn, increase your distance. Perhaps more importantly, the distance you hit the ball with each club will be more consistent. You will therefore be far more likely to hit your iron shots close to the flag.

If you wish to hit a particular shot – low, high, draw or fade – it is simply a matter of experimenting with your alignment and ball position. Your basic swing remains unaltered. Once you have achieved a more consistent ball flight, work on these different shots. They allow you to become an even more complete player.

Above all else, be patient with your athletic swing. Great swings are never produced overnight. They require a lot of work. Persevere and the rewards will be yours.

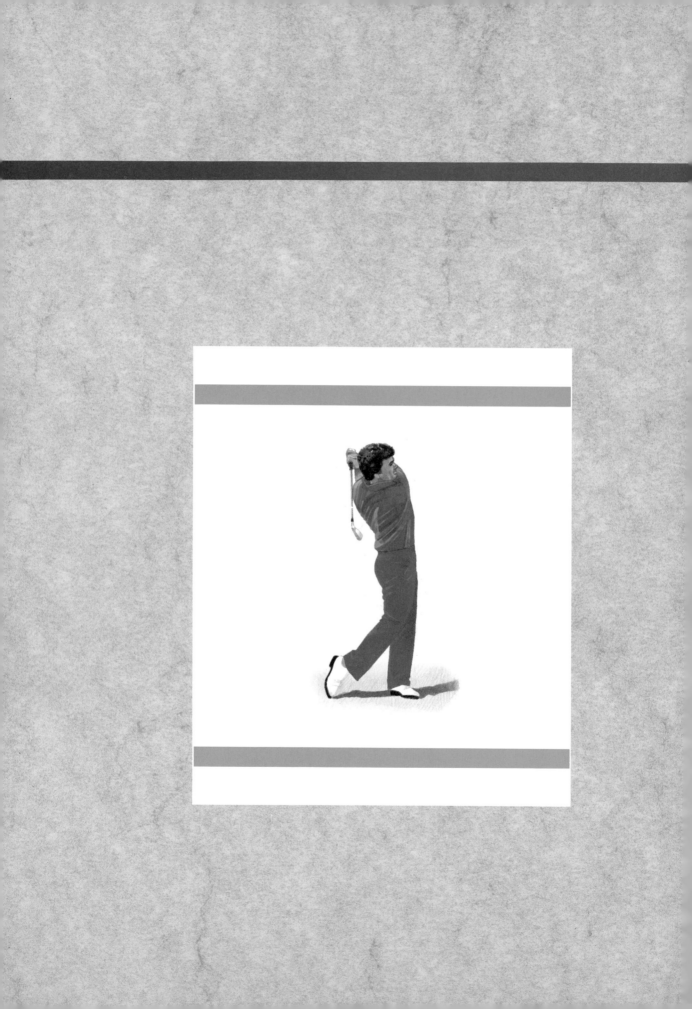

Summary

'CONSISTENCY CAN ONLY
BE ACHIEVED THROUGH
KNOWLEDGE, PATIENCE
AND PRACTICE.'

Summary

The club is placed diagonally across the palm of the left hand and down through the fingers of the right hand.

In your completed grip, the lifeline of the right hand is placed over the left thumb, which itself is placed on top of the shaft. The angles formed at the base of each wrist are fairly symmetrical. The pressure exerted by each hand should be roughly equal – light but firm.

At address you are in a 'ready' position: both feet comfortably turned out at approximately 30 degrees, the ball opposite your left armpit. You are ready to swing the club away.

The test for good posture is being able to have an imaginary line pass through the middle of the right tricep or shoulder down through the kneecap into the ball of the foot.

Aligning the clubface squarely is the first step towards aligning the body to the target. As an aid to that alignment, place three clubs on the ground parallel to one another; one along your toeline, one pointing from the ball to the target and one outside the ball. Your feet, knees, hips and eyes should be parallel to these lines. The shoulders, however, are a little open so that the lower half of the left forearm is visible when viewed from behind.

Use the 'criss-cross' drill, right hand on left shoulder, left hand
on right shoulder, to simulate the correct pivot motion.
(In making this pivot motion, be sure to maintain
a constant spine angle.)

On the backswing, you must turn around your right axis point,
an imaginary line extending down from your right armpit.
On the downswing the same thing happens, only around
your left axis point.

As you turn and coil around your right axis point on the backswing, the flex created in your right knee at address *must* be maintained.

During the transition stage of your athletic swing, your legs should assume a squat, 'sit-down' look.

The change of direction can be felt by placing a club behind your shoulders.

(a) Link one in your athletic swing is address.

(b) At link two, your clubhead points at eight o'clock on an imaginary clockface. The butt end of the club, which is over the middle of your right thigh, points at your navel.

(c) If link two was eight o'clock, link three is nine o'clock. Here your club should be parallel to the ground and parallel to the target line. Imagine that the palm of your right hand is in a 'shake hands' position.

(d) At link four your left arm is horizontal. The club has also shifted onto a slightly more upright plane. From here on it is merely the turning motion of your body that will carry the club to the end of your backswing.

133

(e) Link five is, in effect, link four transferred to the 'top' by the completion of your pivot action. Your left arm rides up your chest, but the two still remain closely attached.

(f) Another transfer: this time your transition moves link five to link six. The downswing plane, however, is now flatter than that going back. Again, there is no lessening of the relationship between your left arm and chest – the two remain closely linked.

134

(g) Link seven is a virtual mirror image of link three. The club is again parallel to the ground and parallel to the target line. Your wrists are still fully cocked in what I call the 'delivery' position.

(h) At impact in link eight, your main goal must be to return the shaft of the club to the position and angle it assumed at address. Then the club is 'planed' and you are more likely to hit a solid shot. Note, too, that your spine angle is also the same as that at address.

135

(i) Link nine is another mirror image, this time of link two. Here, however, the club is pointing at four o'clock, not eight. The linkage between your arms and body is still evident, the butt end of the club pointing at your navel.

(j) At link ten, your right arm is fully extended just past horizontal, placing your wrists in the fully hinged position they filled at link four. Your body should have rotated almost fully until you are facing the target.

(k) Link eleven is merely an extension of link ten. Your arms are carried to the end of your swing by the completion of your pivot.

The first move of the club is not solely attributable to your hands and arms. Simulate the move away of your club by placing the shaft in your navel and turning until it points at eight o'clock. Feel how your body has initiated the turn in order to start the club away. The body must move the club.

Think of your athletic golf swing as a mirror image, passing through similar positions on either side of your body.

The plane of your backswing is steeper than that of your downswing.

The 'top' of the backswing is a useful reference point, but it is not a static position. In fact, at the 'top' your body is actually moving in two directions at once. As your upper body completes its backward move, your lower body is already moving towards the target.

At impact, imagine that you are hitting into a wall.

Make some swings with your right arm only. This emphasizes that it is your right side which ultimately releases the clubhead through the ball.

If you can hold your finish position for a few seconds, then you have
swung in balance.

And finally, the full athletic golf swing.